CONSECRATED UNTO ME

Behold, thou art consecrated unto me by this ring as my wife, in accordance with the faith of Moses and of Israel.

From the traditional
Jewish marriage ceremony

Illustrated by William B. Steinel

UNION OF AMERICAN HEBREW CONGREGATIONS

CONSECRATED UNTO ME

A JEWISH VIEW OF LOVE AND MARRIAGE

by Rabbi Roland B. Gittelsohn

NEW YORK, N.Y.

Library of Congress
Catalog Card No. 65-24635

TO

**Donna and David
Judith and Richard**

May their love be consecrated anew each day.

EDITOR'S INTRODUCTION

IN RESPONSE TO A CALL FROM CONCERNED PARENTS AND RABBIS, AN
ever-increasing number of religious schools are offering confirmation or high school courses on "Judaism's Personal Values," a
prominent feature of which are units of instruction on sex and the
Jewish perspective of the complex problems associated with it.

Our young people, too, express their need and desire to have
religious guidance in this realm. They point out that contrary to
the prevailing view, most public schools do *not* have any kind of
planned sex education. An occasional movie or a single lecture by
a visiting doctor or psychiatrist is about the best that can be expected, and even then only the biological aspects of sex are discussed, and not the moral responsibilities that go with it. It is this
wider perspective which our children want and which the religious
school is uniquely equipped to offer.

Roland B. Gittelsohn's *Consecrated Unto Me* provides us with
the much-needed text on the subject. It is an excellent work that
reflects not only the author's considerable knowledge and creative
skills; it is also the product of better than a decade of experience in
teaching courses on the "Jewish View of Love and Marriage" to his
confirmands. He approaches all aspects of the boy-girl, man-woman
relationships with candor and understanding, and in the light of

all that is known concerning them from every available area of knowledge and experience.

Properly, the book focuses beyond the biological to the moral issues involved, and in this process brings to bear what Judaism has to say. Problems of particular concern to the contemporary Jewish community—interdating and intermarriage—are also given appropriate consideration.

Consecrated Unto Me will help the teacher in his work and the student in his life. Hopefully, also, the availability of this text will impel an even greater number of congregations to introduce courses on the subject—both in the formal setting of the classroom and in the informal education program of the youth group and of our camps.

Our adolescents have the right to look to us for guidance as they struggle to refine standards of conduct in their personal and communal lives. We should be prepared to help them find their way through the maze of eroticism which bewilders them to the true meaning of love for which they yearn.

RABBI ALEXANDER M. SCHINDLER

PREFACE

I AM INDEBTED FAR BEYOND MY UTMOST CAPACITY OF EXPRESSION TO loving friends, without whose generous assistance this volume would have remained an idle dream.

Foremost among these are the several hundred high school juniors and seniors who have been my students at Temple Israel of Boston. Their response to my unit of instruction in "Preparation for Marriage" has encouraged me to expand my notes and to make them available in this form to young people elsewhere. Two of my students in particular—Susan Kotlier and John Levy—read the manuscript with uncommon skill, giving me the honest reaction of the age group for which these chapters are intended.

Rabbi Alexander M. Schindler—Director of the Commission on Jewish Education—provided unlimited assistance and advice. Other readers on behalf of the Commission were Mrs. M. Myer Singer, Rayanna Simons, and Rabbis David Hachen, Henry Skirball, Leon Fram, Samuel Glasner and Jack Stern, Jr. They are all very busy individuals; the promptness and thoroughness of their criticisms are deeply appreciated. The attractive format which so effectively enhances the content of this book is the work of Mr. Ralph Davis.

I am equally grateful to a corps of personal readers. Because there is much material of a technical nature in these pages, I called upon each of them to render judgment in the field of his own special competence. They were more than generous in their response—Dr. Sidney Slater Cohen as an obstetrician and gynecologist, Dr. Herbert I. Posin as a psychiatrist and Professor F. Alexander Magoun as a marriage counselor.

Neither time nor fatigue was an obstacle to my devoted secretary, Miss Bessie R. Berman, in her several typings of this work. Through the years she has developed an uncanny capacity to piece together into a sensible sequence the many sheets of paper, the countless cards and inserts, on which my thoughts and afterthoughts are so confusingly interlaced.

My beloved wife played a double role in the birth of this book. It is her love for me and mine for her that makes it possible for me to offer my students a view of marriage at its best. And her patient acceptance of neglect when the writing went well, of irascibility when it went poorly, enabled me to complete the work without too heavy a burden of guilt.

As *Consecrated Unto Me* is offered to the public, my hope is a simple one. May an insight here, a suggestion or comment there, touch the hearts and minds of many among my readers—helping them to a higher evaluation of themselves and a more wonderfully happy marriage!

ROLAND B. GITTELSOHN

CONTENTS

CONSECRATED
UNTO ME

Chapter ONE

MARRIAGE: HEAVEN OR HELL?

THE MOST IMPORTANT DECISIONS YOU WILL EVER HAVE TO MAKE ARE your choice of a vocation and of a husband or wife. Of the two, there can be little doubt that the second is even more significant than the first. The man or woman who enjoys a happy marriage can, if necessary, adjust himself to the unavoidable difficulties of his vocation, or can even change his profession or job. The husband or wife who is trapped in the wrong kind of marriage may drive himself mercilessly to compensate with satisfactions elsewhere, but will almost certainly fail to find them. No matter how immersed you may eventually be in your vocation, it will occupy and challenge only a part of you. Your marriage, on the contrary, will involve the whole of your personality—your physical being, your intellect, your emotions, your spiritual capacities—everything!

3

There is no other experience or relationship quite like marriage. It can bring us the most exalted happiness—or the most miserable distress—of which we humans are capable. The negative possibilities of marriage are illustrated by the following excerpts from a news story which appeared in the *Miami Herald* of March 2, 1964:

I GOT A TELEGRAM SAYING HE DIED

Edward Hallenbeck spoke in broken cadences of grief:

"All I know is I got a telegram saying he died. I don't know what happened. They said she inflicted the wounds." His son, Terry, 23, an Air Force enlisted man, was stabbed to death Wednesday in Sunnyvale, Calif. The young airman's bride of four days, Mary Ann, 21, was arrested and charged with murder. . . .

Police said young Hallenbeck was stabbed as he unpacked in the couple's honeymoon apartment. The weapon was a seven-inch carving knife, a wedding present.

He died two hours later in a hospital.

Police said Mrs. Hallenbeck told them after her arrest, "I just had to do it."

How can we account for this unspeakable tragedy? Did Terry reveal himself to be a cruel and sadistic groom? Was the young bride unable to face the responsibilities of marriage? Did she find her first sexual encounter with her husband intolerable? We have no way of knowing.

It could have been any one of these answers, or a hundred others. What we do know is that, though this is an extreme and fortunately a rare kind of occurrence, it does occasionally happen, and it demonstrates the abysmal misery which some couples find in marriage. Not all marriage failures are as horrifying as that of Mary Ann and Terry. Many couples remain married for life, but one or the other partner comes to feel that he or she was trapped, that with a wiser choice of mate, life could have been a completely different and happier reality.

The husband and wife who are divorced after some years of marriage, or who maintain the appearance of a successful marriage despite the fact that both are miserable, constitute a truer and more common example of marital failure than do the Hallenbecks. They—and their children—also suffer a good deal more, even if less dramatically. There is probably no greater cause of unhappiness and emotional distress among children than parents whose marriage has failed.

Others find sublime happiness in marriage. One man said on his thirtieth wedding anniversary: "The luckiest event in my whole life was marrying my wife. Sure, we have had plenty of problems. There have been times when we quarreled and perhaps even acted temporarily in unloving ways toward each other. But neither of us could ever have become the person he is today without the love and encouragement of the other. God's greatest blessing to us has been our love for each other and the opportunity to express this love in our marriage." His wife—too choked up with emotion at the moment to risk any verbal comment—expressed her agreement with the silent eloquence of her eyes.

There is a peculiar paradox here. Though marriage is the most crucial decision we face, though it has the potential of bringing us so much happiness or sorrow, it is one of the few important choices in life for which no preparation is required by law. To become a craftsman, one must first serve as an apprentice. To qualify as a physician or attorney or accountant, one must go through a rigorous course of preparation. To obtain employment as a beautician or barber, one must demonstrate ability and receive a franchise from the city or state. To drive an automobile one must qualify by taking a test. But to secure a marriage license, all one needs is the required amount of money and, in most states, a blood test. We can only speculate on how much of the unhappiness which some couples experience could be avoided with proper education before marriage.

Both science and Judaism have something to say about the circumstances and conditions which can increase the probability of success in marriage. The purpose of this book is to transmit to you the insights of both science and Judaism, to stimulate your own best thinking on marriage, and to provide the kind of knowledge which Terry and his bride obviously lacked.

Why Now?

This, of course, is not the beginning of your education about marriage and sex. In actual fact that education commenced long before you were aware of it. When your mother first held you in her arms as an infant, you were learning something about love and the pleasures which physical contact can bring to people who love each other. When you observed the manner in which your parents acted toward each other in your home, you were learning many things—perhaps some good, some bad—about love. When you first discovered that certain parts of your body were more sensitive than others, you were beginning to learn important lessons about sex. Your education in this area has been going on since the moment of your birth.

Unfortunately, not all of it has been good. If you are typical of your contemporaries, your parents and teachers have been reluctant to give you the information and attitudes you need; you have been forced to obtain at least some of your information from friends, never fully knowing whether or not that information is accurate. A 1938 survey conducted by the American Youth Commission indicated that only thirty per cent of the young people queried had received most of their sex education from their parents. A later study, made in the early 1960's, showed encouraging improvement, but still not more than about forty per cent reported their parents as their primary source of information and knowledge concerning sex.

The more recent study showed that two-thirds of the boys and forty per cent of the girls had received most of their sex facts from friends their own age. Needless to say, too often such "education" amounts to little more than the blind leading the blind. College freshmen were asked which topics they found most difficult to discuss with their parents. Eighty-five per cent answered sex— eighty per cent petting—almost as many listed love, courtship and marriage. Even at this level, between a third and a half admitted that most of their information in these areas had come from friends.[1] Intelligent decisions are possible—concerning both marriage and the sex problems you face now—only when based on knowledge which is reliable and accurate.

If you are among the fortunate few whose parents have felt comfortable enough in their own family and sex lives to discuss these subjects with you fully and freely, you have a head start toward acquiring such knowledge. In any event, however, it is possible that there are areas not covered, misconceptions which await correction, and questions which remain unanswered. Some parents—much as they would like to help their sons and daughters—find themselves unable to do so because they themselves were not adequately informed in their own youth.

There is a further reason why this is precisely the time in your life when questions of love, sex, marriage and the family must be faced. It is during the high school and early college years that most young people begin to feel most urgently a whole host of sensations, desires, needs and fears growing out of their sexual development. More and more marriages are taking place at this early age. And even for those who postpone any serious thought of marriage until later, there is evidence that very few men or women later change the type of sex behavior they establish for themselves at this stage of their lives. The kind of relationship you develop now with the opposite sex, your dating habits, your attitudes and conduct with regard to petting—all these will have a direct bearing on the success of your marriage. In short, enough is at stake—in terms of your present needs and doubts as well as your eventual happiness as a husband or wife—to make the concerns of this book among the most important you face.

For Instance

The purpose of this book is not only to deal with theory, but also to help you face and solve the kinds of problems people actually encounter in connection with marriage and family life. For this reason, at the end of each chapter you will find several cases illustrating the points of that particular chapter. In your class or discussion group these cases will be explored in depth. In order to arrive at an intelligent opinion of your own, it is essential that you read the entire chapter carefully and also think about it before the discussion. While all these cases are fictional, there is no problem or situation described in them with which the author has not actually been confronted in his professional career.

A. David and Doris have known each other since their freshman year of high school. For several years they were only casual friends; for the past two years they have dated only each other. David, who is 22, is eight months older than Doris. Both are now seniors at the same college. When they are graduated in June, David hopes to enter medical school, while Doris anticipates a teaching career. David's parents, who are wealthy, are prepared to finance his medical education but they are unhappy over the couple's desire to be married at the end of the year. Their principal objections are that Doris' parents are divorced and that she is a Protestant while they are Catholics. Both young people are convinced they can handle the religious disparity without too much trouble. They feel their love is sufficiently strong so that when children are born to them, they will then be able to agree on the religion the children are to follow.

Because they attend the same college, David and Doris have been able to see each other almost daily. They enjoy skiing together in the winter, swimming and golfing in the summer. Both love opera and symphonic music, neither cares very much for museums. They agree on having a family of about three or four children and on spending more money for books, records and travel than on clothing and social pursuits.

> What positive factors do you see which would point to probable success for David and Doris in their marriage? What negative factors which might lead to failure? Would you recommend that they proceed as they have planned? Why? How would you feel if you were their parents?

B. Bill and Frances fell madly in love the very first time they met on a blind date four months ago. They have been together practically every evening since. Frances' mother is worried over their interest in each other, chiefly because Bill is 34 while Frances is only 20. She is trying not to be selfish, however, realizing that her view could be colored by the fact that since her husband died eight years ago Frances has been the focus of all her attention and love at home; there are no other children. Bill has tried to reassure Mrs. Ames by promising that after they are married she will be welcome to live with them.

Before meeting Bill, Frances enjoyed nothing more than curling up before the fireplace with a good book. She has done little reading recently; Bill prefers to spend their evenings together bowling or dancing, and in order to please him she has raised no serious objection. She feels very safe and secure when with him. He seems to know the right answer whenever she herself is in doubt. He is able and willing to make decisions without troubling her.

The one thing in their relationship which bothers Frances considerably is the matter of sex. They have kissed frequently, but several times Bill has wanted to pet. Her mother has continually told her that a nice girl does not allow a man to take liberties with her, and thus far Frances has followed her advice and has successfully kept their conduct under control. She is very much concerned and afraid, however, of her own strong sexual desires and also worried that if she persists in saying no to Bill, she may lose him.

> What positive factors do you see which would point to probable success for Bill and Frances in their marriage? What negative factors which might lead to failure? Would you recommend that they proceed as they have planned? Why? Which of the two couples described in these cases has the better chance for a happy marriage? Why?

Chapter TWO

WHAT IS LOVE?

"I love my school . . ."

"I love my wife . . ."

"I love oranges . . ."

"I love my brother . . ."

YOU HAVE PROBABLY HEARD EACH OF THESE STATEMENTS MADE, though in each the word *love* is obviously used in quite a different sense. This illustrates how many varied meanings the word is given, and how very difficult it is to define. For our purpose, we are interested chiefly in one special kind of love: that which unites a man and a woman in the permanent relationship of marriage.

10

This kind of love, to be sure, is closely connected with other kinds. Indeed, it is doubtful whether a person who did not receive adequate love from his parents and did not learn to give love to brothers or sisters or friends is capable of fully loving a husband or wife. But we shall limit ourselves here to the *man-woman-marriage* kind of love.

Even when thus simplified, a definition is difficult. There is a story of a teacher who asked her children to draw pictures of what they wanted to be when they became adults. As they busily followed her instructions, she walked up and down the aisles to examine their work. Coming to one little girl who sat before a blank piece of paper, she said: "Mary, I guess you don't know what you want to be." To which Mary at once replied: "O yes, Miss Martin, I do know. I want to be married, but I don't know how to draw it!" Similarly, even individuals who have experienced love as the most wonderfully compelling reality of their lives often find it impossible to describe in words.

Many attempts have been made. Professor F. Alexander Magoun, who pioneered years ago in teaching college marriage courses, has suggested two possible definitions which are worth our consideration. After first rejecting the humorous definition that love is "an itchy feeling around the heart that you can't scratch," he offers the following alternatives:

> 1. Love is a feeling of tenderness and devotion towards someone, so profound that to share that individual's joys, anticipations, sorrows and pain is the very essence of living.
>
> 2. Love is the . . . desire on the part of two or more people to produce together the conditions under which each can be and spontaneously express his real self; to produce together an intellectual soil and an emotional climate in which each can flourish far superior to what either could achieve alone.[1]

How do you react to these proposed definitions? Which, in your judgment, is better? Why? What, if anything, needs to be added to complete our definition of love? Judged by these statements, do you think your parents have had a good love relationship? The parents of your friends? Have you yourself ever experienced toward another person feelings which meet the requirements of either definition above? Do any of Professor Magoun's words or ideas surprise you?

If any do, it might well be the thought that persons in love want to share each other's *sorrows* and *pains* as well as their joys. Yet this is truly an important aspect of mature love. One who expects to share only the happiness of another, while receiving from him strength to surmount his own weaknesses and fears, possesses a most immature concept of love.

It is important to note the implication in the second definition that neither partner in a genuine love relationship is expected to surrender altogether his own individuality or needs. Given two normal persons, it is seldom, if ever, possible to have a good marriage when one partner is constantly sacrificing himself for the other. A martyr is not likely to be a successful husband or wife. (Or, for that matter, a good parent.) Paradoxical as it may at first seem, the person who habitually and fully submits to his mate does not demonstrate true love. To be sure, each partner in marriage will, many times, sacrifice something he very much wants for himself in order that his mate might achieve satisfaction. But in a good marriage both will be making such sacrifices—probably with about equal frequency—and the one who renounces his own desires at a given moment will feel that in the long run he thereby gains far more than he loses.

Love is largely a matter of right emotional relationships. Perhaps an analogy or two will help. Hydrogen and oxygen must exist in the right relationship to each other in order to form water. If, instead of two hydrogen atoms and one oxygen atom, we had one hydrogen atom and two oxygen atoms, the result would not be water. Similarly, the various parts of a watch must be located and operating in the right relationship for one to have a timepiece which functions. If the spring is too large or too small, too strong or too weak, in comparison to the other parts, the watch will not work. If all the parts, though they be of the proper size, are thrown into an envelope but not installed in the right interrelationship, everything physically necessary for a watch will be in the envelope, yet there will be no watch. In each of these analogies, the sum total of the parts in right relationship to each other is more than the sum total of unorganized parts.

Water is more than just hydrogen plux oxygen. A watch is more than just the parts of which it consists. And a couple in love becomes more than one man plus one woman. The man becomes a better man, the woman becomes a happier woman—because of their loving relationship—than either could have become without the other.

A Common Mistake

Very often love is confused with romance or infatuation. You know the usual Hollywood pattern: gorgeous, glamorous female meets handsome, heroic male . . . they dance once to soft music under the stars . . . know at once that each is meant for the other . . . it's love at first sight and they live happily ever after. Or do they? That depends on whether the question applies to an imaginary role or the real life of the movie stars.

There is no such thing as love at first sight. There can indeed be romance at first sight, attraction or infatuation at first sight, but not love! Infatuation is a lower level of experience than love. It can sometimes develop into love, though more often it does not. Even when it does, only the passage of a considerable amount of time can prove this conclusively. Meanwhile, the problem becomes frustrating and dangerous in many cases because, in a young person especially, it is so very difficult to distinguish the two; for the early manifestations and sensations of infatuation and love are exasperatingly similar. The overwhelming probability is that whatever strong emotional bonds a high school boy or girl has felt toward a contemporary of the opposite sex have been infatuation, rather than love. Because far too many couples fail to distinguish between the two feelings in time to avert disappointment and tragedy, it is vital for us to think about the differences. There are primarily four.

1. The first is the test of time. Love has an enduring quality which infatuation lacks. Infatuation is like a match touched to a pile of

A LASTING LOVE

combustible brush. The flame catches at once, bursts immediately into frightening fullness which gives the appearance of lasting forever, then quickly subsides and dies. Love is more like a fire built from small beginnings; first, a few pieces of kindling, then larger logs to build the flame, steady replenishment when needed, glowing coals to warm oneself for many hours.

The following diagram may help indicate the difference. Except for the rare instance where infatuation leads to love, it begins more dramatically, develops far more rapidly, and expires while love may still be incubating.

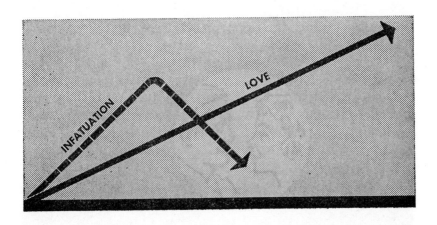

2. A second way of distinguishing infatuation from love is to see whether the emphasis is on the self or the other person, on getting or on giving. The man who is infatuated is really mostly interested in himself; the object of his infatuation is important only for what she can give him. The frame of reference is: *how-much-pleasure-it-gives-me-to-be-with-you.* The man who is truly in love is at least as interested in his mate as in himself; he becomes more important to himself in proportion to what he is able to give to or do for her. The frame of reference is: *how-much-more-adequate-and-secure-each-of-us-feels-because-of-the-other.*

Dr. Harry Stack Sullivan, a well-known psychoanalyst, has said that love begins when one feels another person's needs to be as important as his own.

3. Couples who are infatuated are interested exclusively in themselves. They prefer to spend most of their time alone. While of course those who are in love also like to spend some time only in each other's company, they enjoy being with others, too. Psychologists have helped us understand that there is no such thing as loving only one person in the world. To be sure, the love of husband and wife for each other differs considerably from their love of others, but the fact remains that neither is capable of loving his mate unless he can also love a great many other people.

To love one person in a very special and wonderful way means that, together with that person, I must also want to interest myself in others and do whatever I can for them. Infatuation can be compared to a couple who use a magnifying glass to focus the rays of the sun only on themselves; sooner or later they are likely to be burned. A couple in love tries to direct the sun's rays so that warmth and comfort can be diffused to others, too.

Some of the most beautiful love relationships in history have been between two people whose love for each other prompted them to do generous work for others. Elizabeth and Robert Browning wrote exquisite poetry—each with his own pen, yet each stimulated and encouraged by the other. Marie and Pierre Curie together discovered radium, and with it brought blessing and healing to multitudes. Louise and Stephen Wise established a great synagogue and labored for those less fortunate than themselves. Not all of us possess the genius of couples such as these. But even ordinary husbands and wives—if each is mature and if they truly love each other—bring blessings of warmth and strength into the lives of those who surround them. Apparently, our ancient rabbis understood this special quality of love. They incorporated this story into Midrashic literature:

> There once lived a pious man who was childless. He prayed for a son, vowing to invite to his wedding-feast every poor person in the city. A son was eventually born to him, and he gave him the name of Mattaniah, namely, a gift from God. The boy grew up and his wedding day approached. The father invited all the students of the Torah and all the poor, who together filled six rooms.
>
> God wished to test the bridegroom, and He sent the Angel of Death, in the guise of a man attired in soiled raiment, to beg for a place at the wedding. The bridegroom refused on the plea that all who could be accommodated had been invited. Moreover, the man's garments were objectionable.
>
> In the night the Angel of Death revealed himself, declaring that he was about to take away the bridegroom's soul, since he had failed in the test. The bride gave voice to this prayer: "O Lord of the Universe, Thou hast said in Thy Torah that, when a man takes unto himself a wife, he shall bring her cheer for a full year and not leave her. May it be Thy will that my husband live before Thee, and I shall teach him to practice loving-kindness to everyone without discrimination."
>
> Her prayer was heard on High, and the Angel of Death was commanded to leave.
>
> What was the nature of this young woman? Her mother was accustomed to draw cool water from a

spring for school children. When she became old, her daughter said: "You need not abandon your good deed. I shall lend you the strength of my arm and carry most of the weight so that you may continue to perform the Mitzvah."

It was this consideration for her mother that made her deserving in the eyes of the Lord.[2]

4. Finally, infatuation is a purely physical experience, while love is both physical and spiritual. True, infatuation involves emotions too, but they are less stable and mature than the emotions of love. It is important to note that love is no less physical than infatuation, but where the one is physical *only*, the other is physical *plus*. If the primary or sole interest two people have in each other is physical, if their principal joint activity is petting, we can be sure it is an instance of infatuation, not of love.

The statement, "I love oranges," comes closer to infatuation than to love. It obviously bespeaks an attraction which is purely physical and in which the "lover" intends to destroy the orange and use it for his own benefit. Far too frequently men and women mean this when they mistakenly and immaturely believe themselves to be in love. To say that love is a spiritual as well as a physical experience is to say that there is something sacred in the love of a man and a woman for each other. We shall see in subsequent chapters that this sacredness is precisely what Judaism has always taught.

Meanwhile, there are several fascinating assertions in rabbinic literature which bear on this discussion. One is the talmudic statement: "When love was strong, we could lie, as it were, on the edge of a sword; but now, when love is diminished, a bed sixty ells wide is not broad enough for us."[3]

> What were the rabbis attempting to tell us here? Were they in fact speaking of love or of infatuation? Is it possible for true love to become diminished? What is the relationship between love and hate?

Here are two rabbinic views on the meaning of love which apparently contradict each other:

a. "Love without admonition is not love."[4]
b. "Love is blind to defects."[5]

Which of these statements is more realistic or accurate? Why? Can the two be reconciled?

It is possible to arrange a neat list of the four principal differences between infatuation and love, as we have done in this chapter. To distinguish one from the other in actual experience, however, is far more difficult. The feelings which inundate a person who is infatuated and sexually attracted to another are among the most powerful, indeed at times overwhelming, in human experience. They are so strong that it often becomes almost impossible to think clearly or judge objectively. It is easy to think that one is primarily interested in another rather than oneself, that the emotion one feels is broad enough to encompass many others, and that the relationship is spiritual as well as physical—even when, in fact, none of these suppositions is true. This is why the first test of love—the test of time—becomes in a way the most important test of all. Hasty marriages are almost never a good idea. As we shall see in a later chapter, couples who wait patiently, who give themselves opportunity to apply the test of time, have a much better chance for marital happiness than those who marry in haste.

Adding Up

To summarize, perhaps the closest we can come to a valid definition of love is something like the following: Love is a consuming desire to share one's whole life both physically and spiritually with another person of the opposite sex, to share that person's sorrows and pains no less than his pleasures and joys. In love one is at least as anxious to give as to receive. Love is a relationship in which each partner is able to develop his own abilities and fulfill his own hopes in far greater measure than either could have done alone.

The kind of love described in this chapter makes it desirable and possible for two people to marry and establish a family. Recognizing the supreme importance of this kind of experience, Judaism has had, from its beginnings, many things to say about love, marriage and the family. You have already become acquainted with a few of these Jewish emphases in foregoing pages; in the next chapter we shall meet more of them.

For Instance

A. Grace is in no hurry to marry. She is a very attractive girl and has been popular since her early high school days. Now, at the age of 26, she still receives many calls for dates, accepts as many of them as possible, and enjoys her social life a great deal. She has politely rejected four proposals of marriage, saying each time that her father is the most wonderful man she has ever known and she does not expect to marry until she finds a man as superb as he. Her parents are naturally pleased with her attitude. They agree that their family relationship is an exceptionally close one and that they are able to give Grace a warm and satisfying kind of love. They see no reason for her to gamble by giving up something she knows and needs for something of which she cannot, after all, be sure.

> What do you think of Grace's attitude and that of her parents? When do you think she might be ready for marriage? Does her conduct indicate a greater or lesser degree of security than the average for her circumstances? How great is her capacity for the kind of love discussed in this chapter?

B. Do you recall the case of Frances and Bill, described in Chapter One? Mention was made there of the security Frances felt whenever she was with Bill. Bill encourages her to feel this way. He remembers that when he was a child his mother, who had to carry most of the family burdens because his father was a weak person, lived an unhappy life. And he does not want his wife to face a similar situation. He feels that a man who truly loves his wife will protect her as far as possible from all difficulty. Because of his strong conviction on this, he makes nearly all the important decisions for the two of them. When they are married, he expects to handle all the details of their budget and checking account, giving Frances a generous allowance and sparing her the trouble of managing any money matters. When he faces business reverses or worries, he does not mention them to her; he wants her to be happy. These are some of the reasons Frances feels confident and secure. She is sure they will have a happy life together.

> What would you say appears to be the prognosis for this marriage? How valid is the love between these two people? Does it meet the requirements set forth in this chapter? To what degree do Frances and Bill seem to meet each other's needs?

C. Karl and Jennie had experienced twenty years of happy married life together before she was stricken with a serious and presumably incurable disease. Though there is no danger of imminent death, Jennie is almost completely incapacitated, spending most of her time in bed. On the rare occasions that she is able to leave her bed for a few hours, she must be helped into a wheel-chair and then back to bed. It is five years since they have been able to share any kind of sex life. Karl has been so attentive to her, so solicitous of her needs, that their friends call him a saint. He has given up golf, cards and everything else he formerly enjoyed. Hurrying home from work at the earliest possible moment each day, he sends the nurse away and hovers over Jennie with tender care. Whenever she voices her guilt over the heavy burdens her illness has placed upon him, he interrupts to tell her over and over how much he loves her and how happy he is to care for her.

> Is it possible for two people to remain in love under these circumstances? Does their relationship fulfill the requirements of love discussed in this chapter? Are they mutually meeting each other's needs? Is each helping the other develop his own highest capacities? How would you judge their relationship in the light of what this chapter says about martyrdom?

D. Donald and Jo are so "madly in love" they can scarcely bear being apart. All day long on the job he thinks of her and can barely wait for the evening when they can be together again. They used to date with one or two other couples, but recently find they are spending their evenings more and more alone. Other people just seem to distract their attention and to delay the hour they really desire—the time when they can curl up together in the comfortable living-room chair. The physical attraction between them becomes stronger and stronger. They have necked and petted a lot. While both have some doubts as to the propriety of their behavior together, somehow they seem unable to resist intimate physical contact when they are together. This desire, far from subsiding in the six months they have been in love, grows stronger from day to day. It is this fact more than anything else which convinces both of them that their love is genuine; they wish it were possible for them to marry now, but financial conditions make this impossible for at least another year.

> Is this a case of love or infatuation? Why? Of what significance is the fact that they have felt this way for six months and that their feelings toward each other grow stronger and stronger? Would their situation be better if they were able to marry now?

Chapter THREE

LOVE AND THE FAMILY

MOST OF US HAVE PROBABLY TAKEN OUR FAMILIES FOR GRANTED, precisely because we have always lived as part of them—much as we take the oxygen in our atmosphere for granted because we have breathed it from the instant of birth. But a moment's reflection will convince us that the family is not only one of man's most important institutions, it is a uniquely human invention. There is nothing like the family in animal life. There are, perhaps, prototypes for the clan or tribe in the herds found among certain species of animals, but there is nothing even resembling the family!

One reason for this is that it is only the human infant that remains dependent on his parents for so long a time. In animal life, the newborn needs one or both parents for a matter of weeks, sometimes months, rarely as long as a year or two. Usually the male parent is not aware of his offspring, while the female parent remains with them only so long as she is biologically needed. The human child needs his parents at least through the years of adolescence, sometimes longer. A strong and durable family is the only means of insuring him the prolonged attention he requires.

One of the most impressive pieces of sculpture in London's Tate Gallery is *Family Group* by Henry Moore. It depicts a mother and father holding their child in such delicate and graceful balance that if either one should let go, the child would fall. This is a true representation of the fact that children require the active interest and support of both parents. If either one is absent—by virtue of divorce or death—the other must exert extra effort to compensate for this absence.

This is, however, only part of the story. We observed in the last chapter that a distinguishing feature of love is its spiritual as well as physical dimension. The capacity for spiritual experience is exclusively human. Animals are capable only of physical relationships. True, we can see, in the more highly developed of them, certain incipient emotions, loyalties and attachments, the ability to accept discipline, and other traits which are the beginnings of what later becomes spiritual experience on the human level. But only in man are these potentialities sufficiently developed to be called spiritual; only in man, therefore, is the family possible.

The human family is a product of the kind of love with which we became acquainted in Chapter Two. It results when a man and woman feel so strong a desire to share all aspects of life that they wish to establish an environment in which such sharing will be permanently possible. Hence the family at its best is both a consequence of love and the best means we know of fostering its further development.

The Jewish Family

In no culture or group has the family been so important as in ours. One of the earliest idyllic descriptions of wholesome family life, encompassing three generations, is found in the one-hundred-twenty-eighth Psalm:

Happy is every one that revereth the Lord,
That walketh in His ways.
When thou eatest the labor of thy hands,
Happy shalt thou be, and it shall be well with thee.
Thy wife shall be as a fruitful vine, in the inner-
most parts of thy house;
Thy children like olive plants, round about thy
table.
Behold, surely thus shall the man be blessed
That revereth the Lord.
The Lord bless thee out of Zion;
And see thou the good of Jerusalem all the days of
thy life;
And see thy children's children.

For many centuries this beautiful ideal was the goal of most
Jewish families and was in fact realized by many of them. You may
have read *New Atlantis,* the account by Francis Bacon of a fic-
titious perfect community. In it there was only one Jewish family.
They had been invited to the community to teach the rest of the
inhabitants the qualities of family devotion and love for which the
Jewish people has long been famous.

Sociologists have marvelled at the strength and beauty of Jewish
family life. To this, more than anything else, they have attributed
the fact that rates of juvenile delinquency, intoxication, dope
addiction, sexual immorality and divorce have been substantially
lower among Jews than in any other group. Some have asserted
that the exceptional quality of the Jewish family is due to the
many privations and persecutions our people have suffered. It is
suggested that, because Jews were not accepted in the larger
society, because their lives were insecure and so many satisfactions
outside the family were denied them, they turned to their own
families for compensation.

While this was undeniably a factor, it is far from the full explanation. The excellence of the Jewish family was also created by
factors from within our heritage, by the ideals of family life which
developed as part of the ethical code of Judaism. The modern Jew
who is unaware of these ideals is an impoverished person; doubly
impoverished, because he has forfeited a legitimate source of
pride in being a Jew, and has neglected a possible stimulus to

added happiness in his marriage. One of the tragedies of Jewish life in the United States today is that, because our knowledge of Jewish teaching in this area is less thorough than it once was, the superiority of Jewish family life is now being threatened.

In the summer of 1964 Louis Z. Grant, a Chicago Jewish attorney who has specialized in matrimonial law, declared that there had been a tenfold increase in divorces among Jews during the preceding decade. The greatest proportion of these divorces, he said, were to be found in "the lost generation of Jews, without a proper Jewish education." The principal purpose of this chapter is to review some of our Jewish precepts on marriage and the family, in the hope that they may increase the probability of happiness some day in your own marriage.

Ancient Wisdom

There are numerous indications in Jewish tradition that, long before the advent of modern psychology and marriage counseling, our ancestors were aware of the truths we have already discussed regarding love. They knew that love means a full sharing of life between the lovers, that it provides a fulfillment together for each that would be impossible for either alone. Thus one of our ancient rabbis said: "He who has no wife remains without good, without a helper, without joy, without a blessing . . ." To which a colleague added: "He is not a whole man." And still other rabbis said: "The unmarried man diminishes the likeness of God." In much the same spirit, one of the medieval Jewish mystics declared: "The שכינה Schechinah (God's Spirit) can rest only upon a married man, because an unmarried man is but half a man, and the שכינה does not rest upon that which is imperfect."[1]

> What would you regard as the distinction between a whole man and a half man? Can it be said that every married man is a whole man, while every unmarried man is half a man? What might the rabbis have had in mind when they suggested that the unmarried man "diminishes the likeness of God"?

The completeness and fulfillment which husband and wife can bring to each other was further emphasized by our ancient teachers in their comments on the sadness of either mate losing the other. Thus the Talmud proclaims: "The widower lives in a darkened world."[2] It adds that when a man's wife dies, his steps are shortened, his spine becomes bent and it is as if the Temple had been destroyed in his time. To which Rabbi Samuel bar Nachman added: "For everything there is a substitute except for the wife of one's youth."[3]

The association of God with love, already noted, is of special consequence to Judaism. One legend relates that God creates each soul in two parts. One half He places in the body of a male, the other in the body of a female. And love means that the two halves of one soul, created together and originally meant for each other, are reunited in accordance with God's plan. In another rabbinic legend we are told that God thought His creation of the universe had been completed after he had formed Adam. He was disturbed, however, by a note of discord which marred the harmony of the spheres. An angel whom He sent to investigate reported back that the disturbing sound was Adam's sigh of loneliness. Then God created Eve to be Adam's partner, the discord disappeared, and the work of Creation was really finished. In the same vein, when asked by a Roman woman what God has been doing to keep Himself occupied since Creation was completed, one of the ancient rabbis answered that He spends His time matching couples for marriage.

These are some of the quaint, poetic ways in which the teachers of ancient Judaism expressed their conviction that love is part of the very plan of the universe—not merely an incidental relationship conjured up by man on his own. The same truth can be seen and expressed in modern scientific terms. We tend to think of nature as being harsh and cruel, as indeed it often is. What we too frequently forget is that the beginnings of love may be seen in nature, too. Protons, neutrons and electrons must all remain in the proper proportion and relationship with each other for atoms to exist. Atoms must follow a similar pattern if there are to be molecules. Molecules, in turn, must relate to each other in a manner which could be called cooperative if there are to be cells, cells if there are to be whole organisms, individuals if there are to be tribes and nations, nations if a peaceful world is to survive.

We see this most dramatically in the relationship between cells. Originally there were only single-celled forms of life on the earth. In the course of time, two cells "learned" to remain together in a larger whole; then four, then eight—until, finally, we have organisms which contain many millions of cells. When cells developed a way of remaining together, they also began the process of specialization. At the risk of minor oversimplification, it may be said that one group of cells undertook the responsibility of digestion for the entire organism, freeing another group to assume the responsibility of locomotion, another of reproduction, another of elimination, and so on. Despite the fact that all this took place automatically, with no conscious intent on the part of the cells— what was really occurring is that cells were "learning" to do things for each other. With this ability each individual cell was able to realize itself and its potentialities to a greater degree than any of them could have done alone.

Here, on the crudest, most elementary level of simple biology, is nature's pattern for what later became human love. It would be stretching the truth to call the relationship between cells—or, for that matter, even between animals—love. Yet the fact is that long before the appearance of the first human being on earth, nature demonstrated that it already possessed the potentiality for love, and was moving through evolution in the direction of love. Human love developed out of these earlier relationships just as truly as the human arm and hand developed from the foreleg and paw of earlier animals.

"By this Ring"

Through the centuries, Jewish law underscored the importance of marriage. One talmudic passage rules that the only purpose for which one is permitted to sell a Torah scroll is to make marriage possible for a poor girl who would otherwise be unable to marry for lack of dowry. Another passage states explicitly: "A man shall first take unto himself a wife and then study Torah." We can appreciate these two statements only when we realize that Torah and its study constituted the most precious possession and sacred obligation of the Jew. In ancient Temple days the High Priest was not permitted to perform the most sacred rites of the year, those of atonement on Yom Kippur, unless he was married.[4] It was decreed also that if a marriage and a funeral processional approached an intersection simultaneously, priority was to be given to the former.

Occasionally you may have heard a man say, either facetiously or in earnest, that he preferred to remain single because marriage would mean relinquishing some of his freedom. Evidently some men were of this opinion in talmudic times, too. The rabbis answered them by telling the story of an emperor who said one day to Rabbi Gamaliel:

> Your God is a thief, because it is written (in Genesis): "The Lord God caused a deep sleep to fall upon Adam, and he slept; and He took one of his ribs (to create Eve)." Rabbi Gamaliel's daughter, who had overheard the conversation, asked her father to let her handle the matter. The next day she entered a complaint with the emperor that thieves had broken into her home the night before, taking a silver vessel and leaving a gold one. "Would that such a thief visited me every day!" exclaimed the emperor. The rabbi's daughter at once continued: "Was it not, then, a splendid thing for the first man when a single rib was taken from him and a wife was supplied in its stead?"[5]

There are, indeed, certain restrictions which one voluntarily takes upon oneself in marriage; we would be wise to perceive, however—as our fathers did—that, in the right kind of marriage, what each partner gains is far greater than his loss.

No reward of marriage is greater than parenthood. This, too, is a truth long recognized by Judaism. We are reminded by our rabbis that the very first positive commandment given man by God was: "Be fruitful and multiply and replenish the earth!" (Gen. 1:28) No marriage is considered complete until the couple is blessed with offspring. Among the many sayings that have come down to us are these: "A man is not a complete man if he has no son and daughter. . . . A man without children is like a piece of wood, which though kindled does not burn or give out light. . . . A man with children eats his bread in joy; a man without children eats it in sadness."[6]

Because our rabbis realized the enormous importance of love, they created a marriage ceremony by which men and women could formally declare their feelings for each other and, with the sanction of God and society, begin to establish a family. This ceremony they called קדושין *kiddushin,* a word you will immediately recognize as coming from the same root as the words קדיש *kaddish* and קדוש *kiddush,* hence expressing sanctity or holiness. The blessings recited as part of this ceremony acknowledge God as the Source of Love. The couple drinks from one or two glasses of wine, symbolizing the fact that henceforth they will taste together both the happiness and the sorrow of life. In an Orthodox or Conservative ceremony a כתובה *ketubah* is read—a kind of contract in which the groom accepts certain legal obligations toward his bride. Traditionally the groom placed a gold ring on the bride's finger. As he did this, he declared: הרי את מקדשת לי בטבעת זו כדת משה וישראל —Behold, thou art consecrated unto me by this ring (as my wife), in accordance with the faith of Moses and of Israel."

In many modern ceremonies the bride also places a ring on her groom's finger. The Hebrew formula which the Talmud suggested for her to recite seems never to have been adopted as common practice. Some rabbis today ask the bride simply to repeat the groom's declaration with a change of gender: "Behold, thou art consecrated unto me by this ring (as my husband), in accordance with the faith of Moses and of Israel." Other rabbis direct the bride to address her groom in the words of *Song of Songs:* " דודי לי ואני לו—My beloved is mine and I am his."

Thus from the beginning husband and wife understand that they partake of precious Jewish tradition, that Jewish survival depends on the kind of home they establish, and that they in turn are dependent on Judaism if they are to fulfill the richest potential of their marriage.

The Jewish marriage ceremony is one of simple dignity. In this, as in all other respects, our rabbis resented ostentation and attempted to forbid it. Whenever wealthy parents were inclined to indulge in extravagant wedding ceremonies, the rabbis reminded them that the real religious significance of the occasion must not be obliterated by gaudy tinsel. If a prospective bride lacked the means for a respectable wedding gown, it became the responsibility of the community to provide one. In American Jewish life today this emphasis is needed even more than in the past. Rabbis generally agree that the most appropriate places for a marriage ceremony are one's home or temple. The reception following the ceremony should be dignified and simple. In place of an expensive and ornate celebration, how much better it is for the bride's parents either to help the young couple with the money saved or, if such help is not needed, to contribute to an important philanthropy in honor of their children's happiness.

No Guarantee

One of the most common mistakes made by young people today is the assumption that, merely because they love each other and have participated in a wedding ceremony, a happy life together will follow automatically. The founders and teachers of Judaism were too wise to make that error. They knew that marriage is a priceless opportunity, not a guarantee; that each couple must earn its own happiness by the proper kind of behavior. And in order that Jewish husbands and wives might realize the promise of their love and establish together families that would achieve happiness, our tradition contains a number of important directives.

Here are a few of the injunctions which our rabbinic forebears promulgated:

> —Thy wife has been given to thee in order that thou mayest realize with her life's great plan; she is not thine to vex or grieve. Vex her not, for God notes her tears.
> —A wife is the joy of man's heart.
> —A man should eat less than he can afford, and

should honor his wife and children more than he
can afford.

—A man should be careful not to irritate his wife
and cause her to weep.[7]

—If your wife is short, bend down and whisper to
her.[8]

—He who loves his wife as himself; who honors her
more than himself; who rears his children in the
right path, and who marries them off at the
proper time of their life, concerning him it is
written: And thou wilt know that thy home is
peace.[9]

—Man should ever be mindful of the honor of his
wife for she is responsible for all the blessings
found in his household.

—A man must not cause his wife to weep for God
counts her tears.

—Strive to fulfill your wife's wishes for it is equiva-
lent to doing God's will.[10]

How can we account for the fact that all these instructions
are directed to the husband? Does this mean only he must
act considerately in order for the marriage to succeed? How
about the wife meeting his needs? Does a weeping wife
always mean a bad marriage? Why does one of these quotations stipulate that a man should love his wife "as himself"?
Should he not love her more than himself? What do you
think of this same statement's apparent implication that a
man should honor his wife even more than he loves her?

The following additional rabbinic comments may help you answer
some of these questions:

—When the husband is blessed, his wife is also
blessed thereby.

—A wife who receives love gives love in return; if
she receives anger, she returns anger in equal
measure.[11]

In the same category is the talmudic dictum that the choice of a
new place of residence or of a different profession must be made
jointly by husband and wife. Significantly enough, the only circumstance in which this did not hold was if one of them wished to

live in the Holy Land and the other did not. In that event, the desire of the one who wanted to live in the land of Israel received priority.

Finally, Jewish tradition has long recognized that husband and wife must be sensitive to each other's moods and needs, must be able to perceive them, even without a word from the other. Thus a Chassidic rabbi related this incident:

> A Commander-in-Chief received a message telling him that his main line of defense had been broken by the enemy. He was greatly distressed and his emotions showed plainly on his countenance. His wife heard the nature of the message, and entering her husband's room, she said: "I too at this very moment have received tidings worse than yours."
>
> "And what are they?" inquired the Commander with agitation.
>
> "I have read discouragement on your face," replied the wife. "Loss of courage is worse than loss of defense."[12]

In Spite of All

Our account of traditional and historic Jewish attitudes would be incomplete were we not to say something about the Jewish view of divorce. After all, men and women are not perfect. Despite the high ideals of Judaism and the best efforts of individual husbands and wives, not every marriage has succeeded—either in the past or in our own time. Some religions are unalterably opposed to divorce. They decree that marriage is a permanent covenant which must never be broken. No matter how unhappy two people may be in their marriage, it must be maintained. In certain faiths divorce is prohibited; in others, a couple may be divorced but neither may subsequently marry again.

Judaism agrees that marriage is a sacred enterprise, one into which we should not enter lightly nor with the idea that it can be easily dissolved. The Talmud stipulates that "a man should not marry a woman with the thought in mind that he may divorce her."[13] In our tradition divorce has always been looked upon as a

Love and the Family 33

pathetic tragedy. "He who puts away the wife of his youth, for him God's very altar weeps."[14]

A beautifully poignant and poetic story is told concerning the proposed divorce of one couple. It is based on the talmudic law that a husband whose wife has given him no children in a decade of married life may divorce her.

> There was a woman in Sidon who lived ten years with her husband and had borne no children. They went to R. Simeon b.Yohai and asked to be divorced. He said to them: "As your coming together was with a banquet, so let your separation be with a banquet." They agreed and prepared a large banquet at which the wife made her husband drink more than enough. Before he fell asleep he said to her: "Pick out what is most precious to you in my house, and take it with you to your father's house." What did she do? When he had gone to sleep, she beckoned to her servants and said to them: "Carry him on his mattress to my father's house." In the middle of the night he awakened and said to her: "Whither have I been brought?" She said: "To my father's house." He said to her: "Why have I been brought here?" She replied: "Did you not tell me last night to take what was most precious to me in your house and to go with it to my father's house? There is nothing in the world more precious to me than you."[15]

> What does this story intend to convey to us? What does it demonstrate about Jewish law? Do you think that the inability to have children was a valid ground for divorce? Is it today?

It is clear, then, that in Judaism, marriage has always been deemed a permanent, sacred bond, not to be disturbed or upset for slim cause. Yet our tradition does not prohibit divorce. It recognizes that even more tragic than the separation of husband and wife is their living a life of pretense and deceit. Often couples who have reached the end of the road remain together nonetheless in order to spare their children the consequences of a divorce. Now Judaism is aware of how tragic such consequences can be; children

34   *CONSECRATED UNTO ME*

need a unified home, with discipline and love from both parents, in order to maximize their chance for wholesome development. But a home which is intact physically while broken spiritually, a home which is maintained though husband and wife no longer love each other, perhaps have even come to hate each other, can harm children even more drastically than divorce. This is more than just theory. A study of schoolboys in the state of Washington in the 1950's revealed that intact but quarreling families were more likely to produce delinquents than broken families.[16] Judaism, understanding this, has provided the conditions under which two people whose marriage has failed may seek a separation.

Before examining these conditions, it would be wise to pause for a further word about marriages that have failed. From time to time every rabbi hears of a couple who are not happy in their marriage but think that if they have a child it might help. It almost never does. A successful marriage is a precondition for having children, not a consequence. A child has the right to be born into a happy home. Later we shall see that the time for any troubled person to straighten himself out is before marriage, not afterward. And the time for a shaky marriage to be repaired is before the arrival of children. The appearance of children does not remove troublesome problems; it very often adds new ones.

Now let us turn to the conditions under which Jewish tradition approves divorce. They are first described in the Bible: "When a man taketh a wife and marrieth her, then it cometh to pass if she find no favor in his eyes because he hath found some unseemly thing in her, that he writeth her a bill of divorcement and giveth it in her hand and sendeth her out of his house." (Deut. 24:1) The first thing that will strike you in these words is that they give the privilege of divorce only to the husband. A complicated structure of talmudic law based on this biblical passage shows the same tendency; no direct right of divorce is provided for the wife. The rabbis seem to have been aware of this inequity. Therefore they provided that, in certain circumstances, a wife could petition the court to ask her husband for a divorce, and if right were on her side and he refused, the court was authorized to pressure him until it obtained his assent. Maimonides expressed this principle of Jewish law as follows: "If a woman says, 'My husband is distasteful to me, I cannot live with him,' the court compels the husband to divorce her, because a wife is not a captive."[17] So the possibilities for a woman to obtain a divorce were not quite so one-sided as they first appear.

In Jewish law a woman was entitled to a divorce if her husband refused to have sexual intercourse with her, if he contracted a loathsome disease which she was unable to endure, or if his occupation caused an odor about his person which she could not stand. Also if he treated her cruelly, prohibited her from visiting her parents, changed his religion or was notoriously immoral.

A husband could obtain a divorce if his wife was guilty of adultery, insulted him or his father in his presence, was morally indecent in public, disregarded the ritual laws pertaining to women, or refused to have sexual intercourse with him. If husband and wife agreed mutually that they did not wish to remain married any longer, no further justification was needed; the court was compelled to grant their request. In all cases, however, the rights of the wife to adequate support, stipulated in the כתובה ketubah (marriage contract) which was read during the wedding ceremony, had to be respected.[18]

In Orthodox and Conservative Judaism it is necessary for a couple to obtain a religious as well as a civil divorce. The religious divorce, called a גט get, is issued by a rabbi or rabbinical court. In Reform Judaism the civil divorce is considered sufficient.

Judaism accepts divorce, but only as a last resort. Every possible effort must first be made to correct whatever may be faulty in a marriage, in the hope that it can be preserved. Indeed, reconciling a quarreling couple is considered a great virtue. The story is told of Rabbi Meir, who lectured to the public each Friday evening. A certain woman attended these lectures regularly. Her husband, who was not interested in them himself, objected to the fact that she returned home later than he wished. Finally he banished her from the house in a temper, and said she could not return until she had spat in Rabbi Meir's eye. She spent the week with a neighbor and returned the following Friday to hear the rabbi's lecture again. In the meantime, the rabbi had heard of her husband's unreasonable demand. He called the woman to him before the assembled audience and said: "My eye gives me pain.

Spit into it and it will be relieved." It took considerable persuasion before the woman was willing to comply, but she finally did and her husband, when he heard of it, took her back again. We are not told whether she attended subsequent lectures, or, if she did, how her husband reacted. The point of the story is clear: a great rabbi estimated his own dignity and position to be less important than repairing a broken marriage.[19]

For Instance

A. Fred and Gladys were married eleven years ago. Things seemed to be going well with them for the first few years. Since their financial condition made it necessary for both to work, they planned not to have children too soon. By the time of their fifth anniversary, however, Fred had received a substantial raise in salary, Gladys was able to think of resigning her position, and they decided it was time to have their first child. Despite their desire and effort, Gladys has not conceived. With the passing of time, both have become tense and anxious over the situation, with the result that their sex life together isn't good and they are picking and nagging at each other more than before. Fred appears to be even more disappointed than Gladys over their inability to have a child. He feels that the whole purpose of their marriage is being frustrated. The idea of adopting a child is repugnant to him; he says that if he cannot have a child of his own, he refuses to take someone else's.

Things have finally come to a climax with Fred's request for a divorce. He blames his wife for her failure to conceive, says he is being cheated out of life's greatest privilege, and cites the provision of talmudic law that if a wife fails to become pregnant in ten years of marriage, the husband may ask for a divorce. It is his contention that our rabbis were wise men, that they foresaw a situation such as this and made provision for divorce under these circumstances because they knew such a marriage was no good.

> What advice would you give this couple? Whose fault is it that Gladys has not conceived? Is there anything they could do about it? Can one feel toward an adopted child

as he would toward his own? Is it possible for a childless marriage to be a good one? Is Fred right in invoking Jewish law to resolve this situation? Why?

B. Joan bitterly resents the statements from Jewish tradition given in this chapter to the effect that no one who has not married can be a whole person. She was once in love in her youth, but when that didn't work out successfully, she invested her emotional life in other directions. Now in her 50's, she has become a successful psychiatric social worker, specializing with children. She has written and lectured widely, is recognized as a leader in her profession, derives great satisfaction from the work she has been able to do for deprived and unfortunate children. She insists that she is a more complete person, that she lives a richer, more rewarding life than some of her married friends who are chained to their husbands and homes.

> Is Joan right? Can an unmarried man or woman be a whole person? If so, does this prove that Jewish tradition is in this respect wrong? Is it possible or desirable for a woman to combine marriage with a career?

C. Norman is in his senior year at college, majoring in psychology and planning to get a graduate degree in that field after receiving his diploma in June. He has heard and read a great deal about the alleged superiority of the Jewish family, but is frankly not impressed, despite the fact that he is himself Jewish. In the first place, he points to the fact that his own family life wasn't anything to brag about. He recalls from early childhood that his parents never did get along very well and that the atmosphere of their home had been one of tension and stress. His father had studied Bible and Talmud extensively and attended synagogue services regularly. Yet his knowledge of Jewish family ideals didn't seem to have much effect on his life.

Norman does not deny that the average Jewish family life has been superior to his own. To the extent that this is true, however, he credits it all to compensation. He says that because Jews were restricted to ghettos, prevented from following certain occupations or entering into the larger social life of the community, they had to seek in their homes the satisfactions and gratifications denied them elsewhere. He is convinced that in the free society of America it is only a question of time until the apparent superiority of the Jewish family disappears.

> Do you agree with Norman? Are his conclusions rational or emotional? Is it possible for a person to know Jewish tradition thoroughly, yet not apply it to his own life? Would the experience of Norman's father be a valid reason not to study Bible and Talmud? Is Norman's prognosis for the future of the American Jewish family sound? Why?

D. Dan has been carrying on a heated discussion with his rabbi on the subject of the marriage ceremony. It began when the rabbi lectured to a group of college students on the Jewish wedding ritual. Dan was silent during the discussion period but later wrote his rabbi a letter of objection and has since met with the rabbi several times to exchange views further.

What bothers Dan is the idea that a few words spoken by a clergyman can make legitimate what would otherwise be improper. "What counts" he has insisted over and over again, "is not what ceremony two people expose themselves to, but whether or not they love each other. If they do, it is perfectly proper and right for them to live together. If they don't, no ceremony or ritual can make their life together good." He has also expressed the idea that wedding rituals have been invented by religious leaders throughout history, mainly in order to control people's lives. As far as he is concerned, when the time comes for him to settle down with the girl of his choice, a civil ceremony—or for that matter, none at all—will suffice.

> How much of what Dan has said is correct? How much of it is mistaken? Why? Does the wedding ritual add anything to the relationship between two people? Is there any difference beween a religious and a civil ceremony? Though this next question isn't directly related to the case of Dan— do you agree or disagree with the views of the author regarding the most appropriate places for a wedding ceremony? Why?

Chapter FOUR

A FAMILY IS MORE THAN TWO

OUR RABBIS KNEW, OF COURSE, THAT A FAMILY CONSISTS OF MORE than two people. If they stressed the need for love and consideration between husband and wife so emphatically and repeatedly, it is because they were aware that only on such a foundation could the proper atmosphere be established, which would enable children to grow healthfully. Having established the foundation, they then gave equal thought to the relationship between parents and children, recognizing that mutual obligations must be met if the family is to be firm. Above all, they understood what too many modern parents tend to forget: that unless mother and father speak with one voice to their children, agreeing in their presence on all major family matters, there is little chance for happiness in the home. A Chassidic rabbi voiced this thought perceptively when he said: "If husband and wife quarrel, they cannot raise good children."[1] Perhaps, as happened from time to time with the rabbis of old, he somewhat overstated the case; good children do sometimes result from a home in which there is dissension. But bickering between parents is an obstacle which is at best difficult to overcome.

In addition to establishing an atmosphere of concord and peace, what more specific obligations has Jewish tradition assigned to parents in relationship to their children? First, to discipline them firmly. The Book of Proverbs contains a number of injunctions along this line, among them:

> —Train up a child in the way he should go,
> And even when he is old, he will not depart
> from it.
> —Withhold not correction from the child;
> For though thou beat him with the rod, he will
> not die.

In similar vein the Midrash says: "He who rebukes not his son leads him into delinquency."[2]

Lest you get the impression that Jewish tradition approves unreasoning harshness and sadistic cruelty on the part of parents, we hasten to assure you that the discipline referred to above was to be based on compassion and love. The mood between husband and wife was presumed to overflow, as it were, into their relationship to their children. Discipline tempered by tenderness and compassion was the Jewish ideal. The Midrash helps us appreciate this when it tells us that when God spoke to Moses from the burning bush, fearing that he might be frightened, He spoke to him in the voice of his father!

The greatest responsibility of Jewish parents by far was to teach their children the Torah; not only the five books of Moses as such, but all of Jewish tradition, knowledge, literature and faith. It would be easy to fill the rest of this chapter and several more with quotations which illustrate this truth. Here are just a few:

> —A home where Torah is not heard will not endure.
> —If a man does not teach his son Torah, it is as if he
> had merely created an image.

A Family Is More Than Two 41

—He who teaches his sons and grandsons Torah is
as if he had received it himself at Mount Sinai.

—R. Hiyya b. Abba saw R. Joshua b. Levi hurrying
one morning to take his grandson to school. He
asked him: "Why the haste?" and R. Joshua
answered: "Is it a small thing to stand at Mount
Sinai?"

—He who teaches Torah to children abides with
the שכינה Shechinah.[3]

—R. Huna ate no breakfast until he had taken a boy
to school.

—Jerusalem was destroyed only because the children did not attend school, and loitered in the
streets.[4]

—One is immortal if his descendants study the
Torah.[5]

More Than Words

But our ancestors were perfectly aware of the fact that parents
could give their children no more effective lesson than the example of their own lives. A father who is contemptuous of his
children's dignity can scarcely succeed in teaching them to respect
the rights of others. One who is dishonest in either his personal or
business life cannot impress upon his children the importance of
integrity. Parents who do not take their adult religious responsibilities seriously, who do not strive to learn more about Judaism
cannot hope to achieve much in this direction with their sons and
daughters. Our teachers understood and attempted to express all
this when they said: "Every Jew should so conduct himself that
his sons will rejoice to say: 'The God of my father.' "

Perhaps no one has expressed this truth more eloquently than
several of the Chassidic rabbis. For example:

The Belzer Rabbi commented on the verse in Exodus 10:2—"And that thou mayest tell in the ears of
thy son, and of thy son's son, what I have wrought
upon Egypt, and My signs which I have done
among them; that ye may know that I am the
Lord." It may be remarked that the end of the verse
would have seemed more correct if it had been

expressed thus: "that *they* shall know that I am the Lord." But the verse was intentionally worded "ye" instead of "they" in order to furnish us a lesson. Recount to your sons the wonders of the Lord, but remember that this will have a beneficent influence upon them only if you yourselves recognize that He is the Lord.

A man asked the Kotzker Rabbi to pray for him in order that his sons might study the Torah diligently. He replied: "If your sons will see that you are a diligent student, they will imitate you. But if you neglect your own studies, and merely wish your sons to study, the result will be that they will do likewise when they grow up. They will neglect the Torah themselves and desire that their sons do the studying."

These rabbis were not without a sense of humor as they sought to emphasize the importance of parents setting an example for their children. One of them is reported to have seen a man and his son, both drunk, reeling together in the gutter. He said to his own son: "I envy that father. He has succeeded in his ambition to have a son like himself. But I do not yet know whether you will be like me. See to it that the drunkard does not have better success with his son than I with you."[6]

Ahead of Their Time

One of the most astounding things about the ancient and medieval teachers of Judaism, as we have already had occasion to observe, is the degree to which they anticipated the wisdom of modern psychology on the subject of good family relationships. They knew, for example, how dangerous and destructive it is for parents to play favorites among their children. Several of them noted that this was one of the major causes of the jealousy which Joseph's brothers felt toward him—the fact that he was obviously their father's favorite. The Talmud states quite categorically: "Show no partiality among your sons. Treat all of them alike."[7]

Our ancestors understood, too, that it is primarily the mother who sets the religious tone of the home. According to the Zohar, a medieval book expressive of Jewish mysticism, "The chief influence transforming a man's house into his home is his wife. The שכינה *Shechinah* will not forsake his house if his wife keeps it according to the ways of Israel."[8]

Many centuries earlier the Talmud had given an effective illustration of this truth:

> A pious couple lived together for ten years, and having no children, were divorced. The man married an impious woman and she transformed him into a man of wickedness. The pious woman married a man of wickedness and she transformed him into a man of goodness. Therefore the sages declare: "Woman determines man's behavior."[9]

Another remarkable insight of a Chassidic rabbi seems almost to anticipate conditions today, when so many young couples are married before they are able fully to support themselves, as a consequence of which their parents often provide financial aid. He said:

> A passenger on a ship patiently awaited the day when it would reach port. When the ship was nearing the harbor, a storm drove it back to sea, much to the chagrin of the traveler.
>
> Likewise a man is afflicted with anxiety for his sons and daughters until he succeeds in rearing them to maturity. Then he hopes to be freed from worry regarding their lot. But his oldest son comes with his troubles, seeking paternal counsel and the father's retirement is delayed. The daughter also comes with her problems, and once more his hope of a quiet life is postponed. Few of us are ever entirely free from worry and the necessity of continuous labor in this world.[10]

Finally, another Chassidic rabbi summarized the obligations of parents toward their children and underscored their immense importance in these words: "God treats a man in the same way that the man treats his children. Do not neglect your children, and God will not neglect you."[11]

> What is your evaluation of the responsibilities which Jewish tradition placed upon parents? Were they reasonable and fair? Are any of the responsibilities outlined above no longer valid or important in modern life? Are there any which you think should be added to these?

Other Side of the Coin

Thus far we have attended only to the responsibilities of parents toward their children. It goes without saying, however, that wholesome family life is impossible unless a sense of obligation is reciprocal. Children owe something to their parents too, and the teachers of Judaism were no less sensitive to this aspect of family relationships. The same Book of Proverbs which we quoted on parental duties has much to say about those of children. Among its more memorable quotations are these:

> —A son that dealeth shamefully and reproachfully
> Will despoil his father, and chase away his mother.
> —Hearken unto thy father that begot thee,
> And despise not thy mother when she is old.

Jewish post-biblical tradition is as specific here as we have already found it to be regarding the proper conduct of parents. The Talmud, for example, asks and at once answers:

> In what does reverence for a father consist? In not sitting in his presence, and in not speaking in his presence, and in not contradicting him. Of what does honor for parents consist? In providing for them food and drink, in clothing them, in giving them shoes for their feet, in helping them to enter or leave the house. R. Eliezer said: "Even if his father ordered him to throw a purse of gold into the sea, he should obey him."[12]

A Family Is More Than Two 45

In further comment on the prohibition against contradicting one's parents, the same passage of the Talmud goes on to say that if a father errs on a matter of law, his son should not directly charge him with having made a mistake. Rather let him indirectly and subtly suggest: "Father, in the Law it is written thus"—proceeding to quote the proper biblical or talmudic passage.[13]

A proper respect for one's parents was interpreted as dependent as much on the spirit of one's actions as on the actions themselves. Thus we are told that one man who feeds his father on fattened chickens may not be showing him due consideration, while another who orders his father to do the heavy work of treading the mill may be fulfilling his responsibilities. How is this possible? In the first instance, if the father asks whence the chickens were obtained, the son may impatiently reply: "Eat, old man, eat and be silent!" In the second case, the government may have issued a decree that all millers report at once to the capital. And the son, out of love for his father, directs him to remain at home, doing the relatively safe work there, while he—the son—responds to the greater danger of government labor.[14]

The great devotion due one's parents is manifest in the rabbinic comment that father and mother are partners of God in the proper rearing of a child.[15] It was said that since God knew He would be unable to attend to the needs of each individual child, He created parents to act in His stead. One rabbi proposed that parents are entitled to even more honor than is God. He deduced this from two biblical verses. One stipulates: "Honor God with thy substance" (Proverbs 3:9)—which he interpreted to mean that if one possesses substance, he is to honor God with it, otherwise not. A different Bible verse, however (Exodus 20:12), says: "Honor thy father and thy mother." There are no qualifications or exceptions here; one is to honor his parents regardless of whether he owns anything.[16]

In commenting on the obligations of both parents and children, our rabbis exhibited a profound understanding of the family. They were aware of the fact that if each inhabitant of a household merely tries to get everything possible for himself, without consideration for the others, the result will be a jungle, not a family.

A wholesome family is possible only when each person who is a part of it attempts to find solutions for the problems and meets the needs of all, not just himself.

> Do you agree with all the statements from Jewish tradition here quoted on the obligations of children to their parents? Are there any obligations which should be added to these?

Not Just Theory

Many examples are given of famous rabbis whose behavior toward their parents was considered exemplary. Abimi, for example, was said to have had five sons, all ordained as rabbis. Yet whenever Abimi's father would call him, he would run to open the door, crying out: "Yes, yes, I am coming to you." One day his father asked him for some water. By the time Abimi had come with it his father had fallen asleep. So he stood there patiently until his father awakened and then gave him the water.

One day the mother of Rabbi Tarfon broke her sandal as she walked through the courtyard. In order to save her from walking barefoot, Rabbi Tarfon bent down, putting his hands on the pavement ahead of each step so she could walk on them instead of the cold stones. When he later became ill, his mother asked his colleagues to pray for him, saying: "Pray for my son, Tarfon, for he honors me more than I deserve." When she told them what he had done, their reaction was: "If he had done a thousand times more for you, he would not have shown half the honor for a parent which is commanded in the law!"

In this, as in all other respects, our rabbis were emphatic in asserting that laws and principles are significant only if they be carried out in action. A Chassidic student is said to have observed, in the midst of studying, that his rabbi was deeply engrossed in trying to understand a certain verse he wanted to teach. Knowing from experience that such concentration was usually of long duration, he ran home for his lunch, expecting that he could return before the rabbi would be ready to continue the lesson. As he finished eating, his mother asked him to run an errand for her.

A Family Is More Than Two 47

The boy refused, giving as his excuse that he did not want to delay to the point of missing part of the lesson. On his way back to the school, however, it occurred to him that the whole purpose of studying was to perform good deeds and that helping his mother in fulfillment of a lesson he already knew was more important than hastening to learn another. So he reversed his direction, performed the errand for his mother, and only then returned for his studies. As he entered the room, his rabbi said at once: "You must have done a good deed, for the moment you entered a complicated matter I had not previously understood became clear to me."

The Talmud also tells of a Gentile whose respect for his mother was extreme, particularly in view of the fact that she seems to have been demented and hence very unreasonable and demanding. Once, when he was conducting an important public meeting, she hit him in the face for no reason. When the slipper with which she had struck him fell to the ground, he bent down to pick it up for her. On another occasion she is said to have torn his silken robe, hit him on the head and spat in his face—all in the presence of others. But he neither retaliated nor answered her, in order not to put her to shame.[17]

> How do you react to these directives of Jewish tradition on the responsibilities of children toward their parents? Are they reasonable? Balanced? Fair? Can they serve as a guide for us today? If followed literally, would they improve the quality of our family life? Try to summarize in one paragraph of your own words the responsibilities of children toward their parents as you see them; in another paragraph, those of parents to their children.

There was one important qualification to the high degree of honor and respect which children were enjoined to give their parents. It was conditioned upon the parents themselves fulfilling the requirements of an ethical life. It was deemed to be their most sacred responsibility, as we have already seen, to teach their children the ethical values of Judaism. Only if they did so were they entitled to all the deference described above. And what if they acted in contradiction to these ethical values? A passage in the Talmud is quite clear on this point.

It is possible to think that even if the father ordered his son to defile himself or not to restore a lost article which he had found, he is to obey him; consequently there is a text to teach, "Ye shall fear every man his mother, and his father, and ye shall keep My Sabbaths." (Lev. 19:3) All of you alike are bound to honor Me.[18]

Small wonder, then, that Jewish family life existed on so high a level throughout most of our people's history. Our ancestors were not willing to let the matter rest on general statements, however pious and poetic. They said much on the importance of love and marriage, on the duties which members of the family should fulfill for each other. And they crystallized their eloquent principles into specific directives and laws which every Jew was expected to observe.

Now that we are aware of Jewish tradition, in our next chapter we shall be ready to return to our own generation and to inquire especially into the age at which one is ready for marriage. First, however, a discussion of the following cases will reinforce our understanding of Judaism and enable us to apply its teachings to practical problems.

For Instance

A. When his temple bulletin reprinted the quotation of the Belzer Rabbi given in this chapter, Dr. Allen called his rabbi to object. He felt the implied criticism of himself was unwarranted and that it put him in a bad light with his son, who is a member of the Confirmation class. "It happens," he said to the rabbi, "that I myself do not believe in God and do not practice any of the rituals of Judaism. I have arrived at this position after many years of careful thought. I attend religious services just on the High Holy Days, if my medical practice permits, and even then only to please my wife.

"I have joined the congregation and enrolled my children in the religious school," he continued, "because I want them to know enough about Judaism to accept or reject it on their own when they are old enough. But you have no right to expect me to do anything in which I do not honestly believe. So long as my son and daughter are willing to attend your classes, I shall send them. Should they ever seriously object, however, I tell you right now that I will not jeopardize our happy and peaceful family life by forcing them. Either you accept us on this basis or we shall have to resign from the congregation!"

> Had you been the rabbi, how would you have answered Dr. Allen? Do you think the doctor applies similar standards to all other areas of his relationship to his children? To matters of health, for example? Would it not be hypocritical for him to attend religious services? How would Jewish tradition answer him? How would modern psychology answer him?

B. "It's all very well to stress the importance of studying Torah," says Mrs. Arkberg, "but we have to be practical and realistic. In ancient and medieval times that was just about all a Jewish student had to study. My own grandfather has told me that in his European boyhood he attended a חדר *cheder* (religious elementary school) six days a week, learning every phase of Jewish history, literature and religion. That was the entire content of his education until he came to this country at the age of nineteen.

"But today our children have to study many other things. They need time to do their school work adequately if they are to gain admittance to a good college. They should be acquainted with music and the arts even beyond the formal lessons of school. They must prepare properly for whatever vocation or profession they are to follow. It seems to me that we have to establish priorities and decide just how much time our overly-busy youngsters can afford to give to their religious education. My own feeling is that two hours a week in class is just about the limit and that it is unreasonable to expect them to do homework as well."

> Has Mrs. Arkberg exaggerated the demands made upon children and young people today? Is it true that each person and family must establish educational priorities? Is it impossible for us in modern times to take the emphasis

our ancestors placed on Jewish education seriously? Other than knowledge for its own sake, can Jewish education contribute anything substantial to the welfare of Jewish adolescents and adults? Can it in any way increase the probability of a happy marriage?

C. Jim Starker doesn't argue about the importance of religious education or the responsibility of parents in this direction. He agrees with everything Jewish tradition emphasizes on this subject but says that modern life is so complicated that parents have to divide their responsibilities, with each specializing, so to speak, in certain areas. Religious education he believes to be his wife's department. He travels on business most of the week, comes home Friday evening exhausted, and feels he should be entitled to spend the weekend relaxing and enjoying himself. He assumes the obligation of earning a living and managing family finances, without imposing any of this on his wife, and he sees no reason why she should expect him to share a responsibility which is properly hers.

> Is it true that parental responsibilities are more complicated and difficult than they were in the past? That some of these responsibilities must be carried primarily by one parent or the other? Does Jewish tradition agree that religion is more the field of mothers than of fathers? Would it justify the attitude of Mr. Starker? Who assumes the major part of parental religious responsibility in your home?

D. A feud has been raging for many months between Mr. Bernstein and his college-junior son. It is time for Larry to prepare his application for graduate school. He feels a very strong desire to study engineering. His father, who is a prominent attorney, insists that Larry's field should be law. "After all," says Mr. Bernstein, "you can't deny that I have had many more years of experience than you. I know life better and may even know *you* better than you do. I am therefore in a better position to know where you could lead the most successful kind of life."

Larry's father has also asserted that he is entitled to honor and respect, neither of which his son seems anxious to give him in this matter. He has often cited some of the quotations and examples given in this chapter and has said that what he asks of Larry—for his own good, actually—is less than many great Jews were willing to do for their parents in the past.

The situation has become critical. The two are equally adamant. Larry will not apply for law school. His father told him last night that if he changes his mind, his tuition will be covered by his parents; if he insists on studying engineering, he'll have to be on his own.

> What is your evaluation of this impasse? Who is right? Is it true that Mr. Bernstein has more experience than Larry on which to base a decision? What guidance can either of them receive from Jewish tradition?

Chapter FIVE

OLD ENOUGH TO LOVE?

WE HAVE ALREADY REFERRED TO THE FACT THAT MORE YOUTHFUL marriages are taking place today than in the recent past. There is an interesting cycle to be observed here. In ancient times it was customary for marriages to occur quite early. According to the Talmud, "he who reaches the age of 20 and does not marry, spends all his days in the thought of sin." In post-talmudic times, however, marriage was consistently postponed to a later age, due largely, no doubt, to the fact that life became more complicated. Yet in the last two decades there has been a reversal of this trend, so that again there are many brides and grooms in their early twenties or even late teens. According to United States government statistics published recently, 49.3% of brides marrying for the first time were less than twenty years of age; 40.2% of grooms marrying for the first time were twenty-one or under.[1]

The paradoxical aspect of this phenomenon is its occurrence at a time when in all other respects young people realize the need for more preparation before they are ready to assume full adult responsibility. There is no doubt that today a longer period of education or training is required before one is able to enter a profession, and that the average young person reaches financial self-sufficiency at a later age than did his father. Yet the tendency in marriage has been the opposite. How can we account for this?

There are several valid explanations. For one thing, boys and girls are beginning to date at an earlier age. Many of them therefore start to feel bored with casual social contacts and are anxious for more advanced and sophisticated relationships with the opposite sex. Home pressure is another explanation. In some instances parents—mothers in particular—push their adolescent youngsters—daughters especially—in the direction of marriage faster than they might otherwise be inclined to move. A third possibility is that we live in a time of intense anxiety and tension. The threat of nuclear war, the struggle over civil rights domestically, the many bewildering changes which seem to be imminent in our social and economic structures—all these make our age a challenging but also a threatening time in which to live. Some young people no doubt look toward marriage as a means of reaching for security and assurance.

Fourth among possible explanations is the increased willingness of many parents to subsidize their children in marriage. Only a generation or so ago it was unusual for a young man to think of proposing to a girl until he could reasonably expect to support her. Today a great many couples are married while one or both are still students, with parents assuming a measure of financial obligation until the couple can make it on their own. In other instances, either the wife or both partners work to support themselves until the husband finishes school. A fifth possibility is the increased tendency of high school boys and girls to go steady. We shall have more to say about this a little later; for the time being, we simply note it as another factor in the larger number of marriages at an early age.

Sixth, and finally, mention must be made of the fact that standards of sexual conduct among college and high school young people appear to be looser today than in the past. As a consequence, a certain number of girls become pregnant and find or feel it necessary to marry for that reason. Certain studies indicate that a third to a half of all high school girls who marry are pregnant at the time, while a half to three-fourths of high school grooms are involved in such marriages.[2] No one can really weigh these several factors in order to determine which are of the greatest importance. Nor is it necessary that we do so. Together they account for the larger number of weddings in which both bride and groom are very young.

There have been enough of these marriages so that a number of jokes are already being told about them. One is about the Christian church wedding of an eighteen-year-old groom and a seventeen-year-old bride. When the groom declared to the bride: "With all my worldly goods I thee endow"—his mother turned to his father and said: "There goes Junior's bicycle!"

And Then?

How successful are such marriages? The record is not very encouraging. One authority tells us there are six times as many divorces in marriages where both spouses were under twenty-one at the time of their wedding as when both were over thirty-one.[3]

A recent issue of *Parade Magazine* published a survey of several hundred men and women who had graduated from high school six years earlier. Almost half were married, and almost half of these had married before both partners had reached the age of twenty. Regardless of whether or not they were married at the time of the interview, seven out of ten said they were opposed to early marriages. This even included some who reported themselves to be happy in their wedded life. Barbara McIntyre Gross, who had three children and was separated from her husband said: "At eighteen you're pretty stupid. Maybe I was trying to prove I was grown up. I thought I knew better than my parents, better than everyone."

Samuel R. Porter, who dropped out of college one year after his wedding in 1958, said: "It's the biggest mistake of my life, and I'll regret it for the rest of my life. We should have waited. When I was eighteen, I wouldn't listen. I'm sorry I didn't."

Not all of those interviewed felt this way. Garlynn Rodriguez, who also became a wife at eighteen, said: "I think that marriage matured me more than anything else. Learning to live with some-one else and sharing his life—that makes you grow up much faster."

Two leading experts have summarized their conclusions as fol-lows: "It is our conviction that many persons marry when they are too young, not necessarily in years but in maturity, in experience, and in the ability to meet the many responsibilities of family living. Such marriages are 'bad' marriages, not perhaps because the couple is unsuited to each other, not because of any deficiencies in the persons concerned other than those which time can erase, but because they have assumed life's major responsibility before they were ready to do so. It injures a young horse to do heavy work too soon, the best automobile should not be overtaxed when it is new, a plank breaks when it is overloaded . . . A child should not undertake an adult's job. Marriage means much more than the legality of sharing a common bed."[4]

> What do you feel is the proper age for love and marriage? Is it the same for everyone? Should marriage or a career come first for boys? For girls? Do you think you yourself are old enough to experience genuine love for someone of the opposite sex who is approximately your own age? Have you ever been in love? What do people often refer to as "puppy love"? How does it differ from real love? Should a couple be financially self-sufficient before they marry? In answering this question, consider the following quota-tions from rabbinic literature and decide how valid they are for today.

> —A man should build himself a home, plant him-self a vineyard and then bring into the home a bride. Fools are they who marry while they have no secure livelihood.
> —In olden times the pious Sages were willing to go about hungry, to see their wives and children go hungry, and to devote all their attention to Torah and Mitzvot. God came to their succor and aided

them on their way. In our times, however, there are no such sincere scholars, and they must not rely upon the aid of God if they do nothing for themselves. Nowadays no one should marry until his livelihood is secure.[5]

We Need a Definition

Our discussions thus far on the meaning of love and the importance of marriage must surely have convinced you that only emotionally mature individuals can confidently expect to achieve happiness in wedlock. This brings us face to face with one of the most difficult tasks we shall encounter all through these pages: the attempt to define the word *maturity*. Most of us tend to consider ourselves mature and others immature, without actually pinning down what we mean. Students of human behavior have devoted many hours and innumerable volumes to the subject. Most of them would agree that the following traits distinguish the mature person:

1. He learns from experience and grows as a result of his errors. Being an imperfect human being, he will probably continue to make mistakes the rest of his life, but will, on the whole, successfully avoid repeating the same ones over and over.

2. He willingly assumes responsibility for his own acts. When the outcome is not good, he accepts the blame—without destroying himself and without requiring a scapegoat.

3. There is purpose to his life. He has projected important goals for himself and plans his activities as progressive steps toward the attainment of these goals. Thus he feels fulfilled through growth. He avoids just living each day and making each decision as if it were unrelated to any larger objective.

4. He learns to live with unhappy situations which he can neither change nor honorably avoid. Recognizing that life cannot always be exactly the way he wants it, he distinguishes between those circumstances within his power to improve and those to which he must become reconciled.

5. He accepts himself—his virtues as well as his faults. Since he does not expect to achieve perfection, he need not castigate him-

self for falling short of it. He is able to evaluate realistically both his abilities and his deficiencies. He can accept criticism and disappointment because they are balanced by achievement and success. So long as he has done his best, he does not deem failure a disgrace.

6. He does not need to dominate or control others. There is enough satisfaction for him in improving himself, in exercising his own freedom, so that he gladly extends the same freedom of choice to those whose lives touch his.

7. He is able to defer a pleasure he would like to have now for the sake of a greater joy which cannot come until later and which depends on renouncing the enjoyment which is immediately available.

An emotionally mature person, then, is one who . . . learns from experience . . . assumes responsibility for his own acts . . . moves each day toward fulfilling the larger purposes of his life . . . reconciles himself to even the most unpleasant circumstances and conditions if they are beyond his power, or anyone's, to change . . . accepts himself, his successes as well as his failures . . . feels no need to dominate others . . . is able to postpone something he may want now in favor of greater happiness later.

No one is mature in all these respects and under all circumstances. The best each of us can hope for is to improve, to exhibit greater maturity in these seven directions with each year of chronological growth. Obviously, the more mature two people are, the greater will be the probability of happiness in their marriage.

> Can you think of criteria which have not been included in our list here? Judged by these standards, how mature do you measure yourself to be? How mature are your closest friends? It could be interesting for three or four friends to rate each other and themselves. Use 3 for great maturity, 2 for average and 1 for little maturity on each of the traits we have given; then add up your total and do the same for each of your friends. Each person can learn a lot by comparing his self-rating on maturity to his friends' opinions of him. Don't attempt this, however, if you are too thin-skinned to take honest criticism. No one prerequisite for a happy marriage is more essential than emotional maturity. Hence the extreme importance of understanding

this part of our discussion, as well as the next section in which we try to trace the steps through which such maturity is achieved.

Couples who marry at too early an age often get into trouble because of a failure to measure up very well in maturity. Another source of difficulty is that both are still growing and groping at the time they marry. Neither has really reached his full maturity or defined the permanent goals he will want in life. If, after they are married, the bride and groom continue their maturation in the same direction, a good marriage is possible. If, however, they mature away from rather than toward each other, their chance for happiness is not very great. The closer they are to full development and maximum maturity at the time of the wedding, the more probable is their happiness together.

Harry Golden has commented humorously on the changing values and goals of individuals as they mature. When a girl is eighteen, he said, she asks: "What does he look like?" When she is twenty-five, she wants to know: "What does he do for a living?" By the time she reaches the age of thirty, her question has changed to: "Where is he?"

The Road to Love

Every normal human being is born with the capacity to love and a need for love. We do not achieve the kind of love required for marriage, however, until we have grown successfully through a number of earlier stages. Each stage is typical and adequate at the age at which it appears. Each is dangerous if it persists much beyond its proper time. Here are the levels through which each of us must grow on the road to mature love:

1. *I Love Myself Only*—A tiny infant is at first aware only of himself. His universe extends only as far as his own fingers and toes. Others gradually become important only insofar as they can satisfy his needs. He wants what he wants when he wants it—or else! This stage shouldn't last beyond the age of two years at most.

2. *I Love My Parents*—At a fairly early point in life, the infant begins to become aware of others as existing in their own right.

This process begins with his parents. They become individuals he is able to love for themselves, not just for what they give him. This is normal up to the age of six or seven, is unusual beyond eight.

3. *I Love My Gang Too*—Somewhere along the line each child reaches out for meaningful relationships that go beyond his own home. He becomes part of a group, usually made up of others who are his own age and sex. At this point in his life he is likely to evidence strong antipathy to members of the opposite sex. His personal importance and self-esteem are reinforced by belonging to his gang. Such an attitude as this is characteristic of the early teens, seldom lasts beyond eighteen.

4. *I Like Girls (or Boys)*—The strong aversion to the opposite sex becomes strangely and mysteriously transformed into an equally strong attraction. We suddenly discover that boys (or girls) aren't really as abominable as we had supposed. Therefore we like the opposite sex quite generally—any and all of them.

5. *I Like One Girl (or One Boy)*—The general, diffuse attraction for the opposite sex is narrowed down, after a time, to one particular person at a time. This is the stage of violent "crushes"— with the single object of one's affections probably changing quite frequently.

6. *I Love the Only One*—In due course the field becomes narrowed to one. Having been attracted to all of the opposite sex, then to one particular one at a time, we reach the point of choosing a permanent partner for life.

Now the interesting and significant thing about all this, we repeat, is that each stage is normal and healthy at a given point in our lives. Each, moreover, contributes something to the richness of the next. The more fully one has experienced the earlier levels of love, the readier he is at the proper time to know the meaning of full marital love. The person who has not yet grown through the first five steps is less likely to be ready for marriage. The danger in early marriages is that one or both of the partners may still be in that category. Then trouble is on the horizon.

Most of us never entirely outgrow these earlier stages. From time to time we may be able to detect some trace of an earlier level, usually in something irrational or inappropriate that we have done. This is nothing to worry about, if it happens only on rare occasions. If, however, a person's general behavior is arrested on a level which he should have outgrown, there is reason to fear that he is not ready for marriage.

> How much can you remember in your own life of each stage described above? At which level would you place yourself now? Can you give one example from each period through which you have already passed—to show how you have said or felt or done something within recent months which indicates a residue from that previous period? If you are unable to find illustrations from your own recent experience, try to do so from the behavior of your friends.

One author has summarized the growth from infant self-love to the capacity for mature love, and has at the same time reminded us of our earlier conclusion that real love must encompass more than one's husband or wife. Her words are worth remembering:

> The adult who has successfully come up the ladder of love development eventually reaches a kind of love that affects not only his own dear ones with whom he is in closest contact but in addition many people whom he has never met. He is concerned with his responsibility to mankind. He does things to promote human welfare. He feels warmly toward the men and woman and children whom he meets. He has faith in the power of love that can operate through the life of a really mature person in many ways. While inevitably leading one into hard work and some difficult trials, this kind of love builds character. Its strength comes from an inner peace that enables one to weather life's storms. It can be attained not in a single step but only through the mastery of the other steps of love development that lead to it.[6]

Two Dangers

There are two further possibilities which young couples must guard themselves against as carefully as they can. It happens frequently that—consciously or unconsciously—the prospect of marriage represents an escape-hatch from some situation which appears to be intolerable. Sometimes it's an unhappy home or unpleasant parental pressure. Or it may be a frustrating job—or an inability to decide which of several vocations to follow—or envy of friends who are already married.

Under any of these circumstances, marriage can be not only a means of escape but perhaps also a weapon with which to strike back at the offending party. If a young person knows that his parent is strongly opposed to his being married, what a wonderful opportunity it may be to assert his independence, to get back at the parent for all the abuse—real or alleged—suffered at his hands. One expert describes what sometimes happens:

> How often is this "love" which some feel merely the desire to get away from a quarrelsome, bickering family, a dominating mother, or a tight little office in which one feels stifled? It is understandable that people should strive to get away from that which annoys them, although the basic reasons for the annoyance may be in themselves. When you marry you *assume* responsibilities; you do not *escape* them. A good marriage will mean that life will be much richer and more worth-while, but it will not be easier. Marriage creates as many problems as it solves. The success of your marriage will depend upon what you are getting into, not what you "get away from."[7]

In this connection, let us understand that often young people who are suffering from emotional problems look upon marriage as a possible cure. But a person who is having difficulty handling himself and his problems while single will nearly always experience still greater trouble in marriage. The time to straighten oneself out emotionally is before the wedding, not afterward. Though it is true that the responsibilities of marriage can sometimes contribute to an individual's maturity, it is even truer that maturity already achieved insures a happy marriage.

A second, related danger is that of falling into a bad marriage "on the rebound." A boy or girl who has just been rejected by someone to whom he had been engaged or with whom he had been going steady is often ripe for an unfortunate partnership with someone else. It isn't easy to live through such an experience; to lose a relationship on which one has depended can be very damaging to one's self-esteem and pride. What could be more natural than wanting to fill the void as speedily as possible? Natural, yes—but for that very reason, dangerous! Such an individual is apt to be so anxious to compensate for his recent loss that he fails to consider whether the proposed partner is or is not really the right one for a life-long relationship. We have expert testimony on this point too:

> While you are still somewhat emotionally sore from the last breakup, be unusually careful not to go steady again too soon. It is easy to get caught in the trap of your own feelings at a time like this. You may find yourself hurrying things with some new-found friend, just to prove to yourself that you can win and hold a person of the other sex. This is your pride crying for a little support. You have felt rejected by your old love, so you let yourself in for anything that will comfort your deflated ego.
> You have heard about people who marry for spite. When something happens to break up an old affair, one or the other of the pair rushes into a new union just to show the other that "it did not matter after all." An effort to show your lost lover that you don't care lies back of these plunges into a new affair. What your actions really say is that you did care very much, or you wouldn't be rushing off to prove otherwise. Unfortunately, such hasty unions on the rebound rarely work out. They tend to be grossly unfair to the new partner, and they certainly are no help to either of the persons who have recently stopped going together.[8]

Either of these dangers can be formidable, even when the individuals involved are aware of their motivations. What makes them devilishly difficult—at times even cruelly tragic—is the frequency with which the real dynamics of the behavior are unconscious. When this occurs, it is possible to convince oneself that one is genuinely in love, though such may not be the case at all.

Good rules to follow, therefore, are these: (1) When on the rebound, go slowly. Try not to become emotionally involved again too soon; if you find you are, don't rush into a permanent alliance. Give the old, dependable time-test a chance to work. (2) If you have been generally unhappy about your relationship with parents or others or yourself, be suspicious of any overwhelming emotional attachment to someone of the opposite sex. Be as sure as you can that you are moving *toward* something desirable, not *away from* something unpleasant.

The Question Remains

There is no simple or easy answer to the question this chapter has approached, no one way of determining who is old enough for love. What we do know beyond the slightest doubt is that marriage is serious business, not child's play. We know also that marriage demands emotional maturity and that maturity is not just a matter of age in years and months. One person may be ready for marriage at nineteen, another not ready at thirty-nine. Each must do the most honest, objective job he can of evaluating his own maturity and judging whether he has successfully emerged from the necessary earlier stages of development. Only then has he the right to give serious consideration to marriage.

For Instance

A. "I refuse to be alarmed about youthful marriages or to take too seriously the statistics of divorce in this age group." These were the words of one parent who had read the manuscript of this chapter. She continued: "I married at nineteen and will admit that my husband and I faced pretty rough sledding for a while. But I think I would have confronted the same problems no matter when I married. We have to remember that young people today are biologically ready for marriage long before social conditions permit them to marry. It isn't fair to expect them to live with all their sexual tensions for five or six years; it's better for them to marry than to become promiscuous. Anyway, it seems to me that most students do better after they are married than before. So far as my own children are concerned—though they are now only seven and ten years old—when the time comes, I'm willing for them to marry when young."

> What do you think of this woman's comments? Is it probably true that she herself would have faced the same problems in marriage even at an older age? Is she wise in ignoring the statistics of divorce among young couples? Do you think she would feel differently if her children were ten years older? How do your parents feel on this matter?

B. Rabbi K. was on the spot. Doris and Eddie, two of his favorite young congregants, had appealed to him for support. At the ages of eighteen and twenty-one respectively, they wanted very much to marry. Doris was a freshman in college, Eddie a senior. They had known each other for five years and had been going steady for two. As you may already have suspected, their parents were vigorously opposed to their being married. But they had agreed to invite the rabbi for dinner and listen to his advice.

The young couple argued that each set of parents was prepared to continue supporting their son or daughter through graduate study anyway, and that with little more than what they figured they could get along all right. The parents expressed great fear that Doris especially wasn't old enough for marriage. They were concerned, moreover, as to what would happen if she became pregnant. That might well mean dropping all their study plans and changing the whole course of their lives. When confronted with the divorce statistics mentioned in this chapter, Eddie and Doris said they were aware of the risks but felt sure they would be among the successful couples; they were confident they loved each other enough to surmount all difficulties and problems.

> What advice would you give if you were Rabbi K.? Were the parents realistic in fearing the possibility of pregnancy? If Doris did in fact become pregnant and either or both of them had to drop out of school as a consequence, what effect do you think this might have on their mar-

riage? How much weight should be given to the couple's confidence that they would be different, that they could avoid the risks involved?

C. When Lillian was shown the criteria of maturity described in this chapter, she studied them for a while thoughtfully, then much to her parents' surprise, admitted that she didn't consider herself to be very mature. That, however, did not deter her from being eager to marry Frank at once. For one thing, she said, he was very much more mature than she and therefore could be expected to overcome some of the problems she might be unable to handle. She relied on his strength a great deal. When her parents continued their opposition, she became angry and said that to be perfectly honest, she didn't think they rated too high on these maturity items either, yet they seemed to have remained together all right for twenty-two years. So she was willing to take a chance on being no worse than they. "Anyway," she added, "how do I know I'll be very much more mature in another two or three years; and you certainly wouldn't expect me to wait longer than that, would you?"

> Do you think one partner's maturity can compensate for the other's lack of it? Which of the following would present the best possibility of a happy marriage: (a) two immature individuals; (b) one immature, the other very mature? Had you been one of Lillian's parents, how would you have answered her? What effect do you guess your response would have on her?

D. Norma was an awkward, rather homely girl, who had never been popular with boys. As a matter of fact, she didn't have many girl friends either. She had seldom been asked out on dates; this bothered her a great deal. When she did go out, she felt insecure and unsure of herself.

Last summer Tommie had asked her for a date. It took a lot of courage on his part, for he too had experienced difficulty in social adjustment. He hated to ask a girl for a date because every refusal was a bitter pill to swallow. He and Norma seemed to hit it off well from the start. They dated regularly through the summer and fall, and by spring Tommie had "popped the question." Norma's parents were of course delighted at the favorable turn in her life, but they felt that at nineteen she wasn't yet ready for marriage. To tell the truth, Norma had some doubts herself, though she wouldn't admit them to anyone else. She was afraid, however, that if she turned Tommie down he would stop dating her and she might never have another chance to marry.

How can you explain the fact that these two got along so well as dating partners? Wouldn't that fact seem to indicate they would probably have a successful marriage? What would your advice to Norma be? To Tommie? Were her fears about never having another chance realistic? Is it better for a girl to accept an offer of marriage despite her doubts, or to risk being an "old maid"?

Chapter SIX

HOW TO MAKE THE RIGHT CHOICE

AFTER "HOW CAN I TELL WHETHER I'M REALLY IN LOVE?" THE QUES-
tion most often addressed to experts in marriage is "How can I
choose the right husband or wife?" This is of far greater urgency
to us now than it was at a time when parents arranged matches for
their children. In some cultures, marriages are still arranged by
elders; families couple their respective daughters and sons. The
bride and groom have nothing to say in the matter; sometimes
they don't even see each other until all the plans have been completed.

It has been argued in some quarters that on the whole, this kind
of social structure makes for better marriages than our way of
doing things. This is, we are told, due to the fact that parents are
apt to be more sensitive to such factors as similarity of background

68

and taste and the financial competence of the groom. They are also less likely to permit a daughter to remain permanently unmarried. And finally, being themselves free of romantic attraction in the matter, they can view the two young people in question with greater objectivity than the prospective bride and groom are able to see themselves.

Despite the logic and validity of this contention, there are also obvious advantages to *our* system of self-selection. In any event, it is not probable that in a democratic, humanistic society such as ours, there will be a change in the way we select our mates. Consequently, young people must choose with all the care they can. It would be wise for them to follow the advice of the Talmud: "You may make haste to buy property but you must pause and consider before taking a wife."[1]

Where parents once had everything to say about the selection of their children's mates, today we have swung very nearly full circle to the point where they frequently have nothing to say. Many young people in our culture are notoriously disinclined to follow their parents' advice in this respect. And many a parent has had to learn the lesson our ancient rabbis attributed to King Solomon. They said that he had a beautiful daughter, about whose future he was extremely anxious. He asked once to see in a dream who her husband would be. When his dream revealed that her mate would be one of the poorest lads in the kingdom, Solomon was perturbed. He disapproved of this match and was determined to prevent it.

So he built a palace on an inaccessible island, surrounded it with an impregnable stone wall, and locked his beautiful daughter and her servants in to protect her from her prospective groom.

Sometime thereafter, the young man in question was wandering one cold night in the forest. Lacking enough clothing to keep from freezing, he came upon the carcass of a bull and climbed into it for warmth. As he slept, a huge bird snatched up the carcass, flew with it many miles, and dropped it on the roof of the palace. When the princess went to the roof the following morning, she beheld the handsome young man and at once they fell in love. After a time they were married in the presence of her servants.[2] It would seem that our rabbis were attempting to tell us that not even the heroic efforts of a strong-minded king could prevent his daughter from marrying whomever she would.

In an earlier chapter, we mentioned the rabbinic statement that since God completed the work of Creation He has been matching couples. Here is the full passage embodying that belief—it will help you realize how important the choice of a mate was to our ancestors.

> A matron once asked Rabbi Jose ben Halafta: "What has your God been doing since He finished making the world?" "He has been matching couples in marriage," was the reply . . . The matron declared that she could do as much herself; nothing was easier than to couple any number of slaves with as many slave-girls.
> "You may think it easy," said Rabbi Jose, "but it is as difficult for God as dividing the Red Sea."
> The matron accordingly tried the experiment with a thousand males and as many female slaves, setting them in rows and bidding this man take this woman, etc. The next morning they came to her, one with a broken head, another with gouged-out eyes, a third with a broken leg; one man saying: "I don't want her," and a girl saying: "I don't want him." Thus was the matron constrained to say that the mating of man and woman was a task not unworthy of the intelligence of God.[3]

While we cannot pretend to be God, it is our hope that this chapter may offer wisdom enough to allow you to achieve greater success than the Roman matron. What, then, are some of the things to be remembered in the selection of a mate? We do not suggest that one should walk about with a rating sheet and pencil in hand, scrupulously interviewing each prospect before asking for or accepting a date. The urges which impel young people toward each other are mostly emotional, not calculating and intellectual. But there is a place for reason and good sense even in emotional relationships. Many a marriage has been wrecked on the rocks of failure because the couple concerned never bothered to check their hearts with their heads. The easiest time to think rationally about the qualities in a mate which make for a good marriage is now, before a romantic attachment makes it more complicated to think clearly.

A Difficult Word

What must we look for in the selection of a mate? Much of the answer may be summed up in a single word: compatibility. Unfortunately, however, this is far from an easy word to define. The dictionary defines *compatible* as "capable of existing together" or "congenial." Fire and water are not compatible; fire is extinguished by water; water is evaporated by heat. Some people have as much trouble existing together—especially in the same household—as fire and water. If this is the case, it is imperative that it be discovered before marriage, rather than after.

Usually when a man and a woman are described as being incompatible, it is assumed they are uncongenial sexually. We shall have more to say about this in a later chapter. Meanwhile, there are many other kinds of compatibility on which a good marriage must depend.

1. There is, for example, *intellectual compatibility*. All other things being equal, it is not good for a very bright man to be married to a rather dull girl, or an intelligent girl to be coupled with a stupid boy. Such a match may be exciting for a short while, but it will soon become insufferable. Our rabbis knew this centuries ago. Addressing themselves presumably to one who is himself intelligent, they said:

> A man should sell all he possesses with the object of marrying the daughter of a scholar or giving his daughter in marriage to a scholar. That is like uniting grapes of the vine to grapes of the vine, which is good and acceptable. But let him not marry the daughter of an ignoramus, because that is like uniting grapes of the vine to berries of the bush, which is something ugly and unacceptable.[4]

The *Shulchan Aruch*, sixteenth century code of traditional Jewish law, suggests a hierarchy of values in choosing a mate which reflects the enormous stress put on intelligence.

> A man ought always to strive to win in marriage the daughter of a Torah scholar, and to give his daughter in marriage to a Torah scholar. If he cannot find the daughter of a Torah scholar, let him seek to marry the daughter of renowned communal leaders; if he cannot find one of these, let his choice be the daughter of a congregational leader; if not one of these, then the trustee of a charitable fund; if not one of these, let him select the daughter of an elementary Hebrew teacher, but let him not marry off his daughter to an ignorant man.[5]

2. There is *social compatibility*. It is not snobbery we speak of here, but rather the undeniable fact that, all else being equal, two persons who come from similar social backgrounds stand a better chance for happiness in their marriage than if there is a vast gap between them in this respect. Despite all the fascinating Cinderella-type stories in print and on film, serious studies of marriage show this to be true. With similar social backgrounds, it is more probable that the values and aspirations of two people will also be alike and that the adjustments to be made after the wedding will be less serious than they might otherwise be.

The Talmud seems to have recognized this point, but makes a rather curious comment with regard to it: "It is not wise to take a wife of superior rank—rather go down a step in choosing a wife."[6]

> Do you agree that if there is to be a disparity in social standing between husband and wife, it is better for the male to be somewhat above the female? Why? Would this be as valid today as in talmudic times? Why?

3. *Economic compatibility* is important too. We have in mind here not the financial background and standing of the two families, which would actually be a part of the preceding point, but rather the *attitudes* and *ambitions* of bride and groom regarding

financial matters. If one is a compulsive buyer and the other a habitual saver, this does not augur well—not merely because of the probable dissension between them on money matters, but also because one's feelings about the saving or spending of money disclose a great deal about one's general personality.

Related to this type of compatibility is the question of marrying for money. You may have heard the familiar quip that it's just as easy to fall in love with a rich girl as with a poor one. While this may be true, it introduces other complicating factors. It is certainly questionable whether a good marriage is likely to result if a man deliberately sets out to fall in love with a wealthy girl. And while there is nothing wrong with a girl being concerned about the ability of her future husband to earn a respectable living, if this becomes the overriding factor in her choice, there is reason to doubt the outcome.

Here again, the wisdom of the ancient rabbis was remarkable. The Talmud contains at least two admonitions bearing on this: "He who weds for money will have delinquent offspring." Also: "He who looks for the earnings of his wife sees never a sign of blessing."[7]

> Do you think either the writer of this book or the Talmud exaggerates this aspect of choosing a mate? Would there be a serious problem if one marriage partner was perfectly willing to let the other spend money as extravagantly as he or she pleased, while remaining frugal himself? If there is to be a wide financial disparity between groom and bride, would it make any difference which was the wealthy one? Does financial subsidy from parents help or hinder in making a good marital adjustment? Why? Would it make any difference from which set of parents the help comes?

4. There is a wide variety of *character traits* in which it is important for groom and bride to be compatible. For example, if one is very rigid while the other is permissive and lax, there is probably trouble ahead. If one is punctual and the other careless of time, if one is neat and the other sloppy, if one is an extreme introvert and the other an enthusiastic extrovert, it is easy to anticipate some of the difficulties they almost certainly will have to face.

5. *Cultural tastes* are of equal importance. It would be difficult for a music lover to share his life meaningfully with one who hated music—or perhaps even for an opera lover to be happy with one whose musical tastes run to rock and roll. The future would appear to be bleak if an avid reader married one who never opens a book, or a vigorous athlete were paired with a shrinking, fearful recluse, or a connoisseur of art were attracted to one who hates museums.

> If opposites like those described here were sufficiently attracted to each other to enjoy dating, would that not of itself seem to indicate they have enough in common to make good marriage partners? How could we account for such individuals finding each other interesting for dating in the first place? How about the old adage, "opposites attract"?

6. *Similar interests in children* are also important. Since one of the most important aspects of marriage is rearing a family, it is essential for the two prospective mates to agree on whether they are to have children, how many to have, and in general, to agree on methods of disciplining the children. If you yourself are the product of a home in which your parents frequently disagreed on matters pertaining to your behavior, you will understand how frustrating—even agonizing—this can be from the child's point of view and how vital it is, therefore, to have as much agreement as possible between parents. We have already touched briefly on the importance of husband and wife speaking with a single voice on all matters related to their children. What we have in mind here is agreement on the *attitudes* toward children which underlie their specific statements or actions.

Two individuals who love children appear to have a better outlook for a happy marriage than if one loves children and the other does not. Even two people who both dislike children would seem to have better prospects in this regard than two who strongly disagree—though they would be removing from their lives one of the most exquisite joys of marriage, that of having and loving children.

7. *The more similar two people are in their leisure-time interests, the better for their marriage.* Two of the earliest experts on

marriage estimated that couples who share and enjoy all their outside activities together have fifteen times as much chance for happiness in marriage as do couples who lack such agreement.[8] Would you like, incidentally, to test yourself on this with the next person you date? Pick up the current issue of any magazine or newspaper, go through it together, and find out how many items there are in which both of you are deeply interested—items about which you would like to enter upon a serious discussion.

8. *Compatibility of age* is important, too. While it is impossible to establish an exact mathematical formula, we know that too great an age disparity is not good. A girl who wishes to marry a man fifteen years her senior is apt to be unconsciously searching for a father-substitute, not a husband. A man in that relationship may well be anxious to find a daughter-substitute rather than a wife. Similar unconscious motivations may be at work if the woman is appreciably older than the man. Marriages based on such needs are fraught with danger.

How can one tell whether such explosive unconscious factors are operating in his choice of a mate? It is far from easy to do so. The only reasonably certain way to discover this is through extended psychotherapy in depth. If there are other reasons which suggest the need for such therapy, it should certainly be sought. If this seems to be the only problem of a serious emotional nature you experience, it would be wise to discuss the problem with someone you can trust, someone who knows you and your family well, and who is professionally competent to help you think through the complicated problems involved. That someone could be your rabbi, your physician, a camp counselor or teacher. Any of these would probably be in a position to consider the matter a little more objectively than your parents who are, after all, emotionally involved with you.

It shouldn't surprise you by this time to learn that our ancient rabbis were aware of this problem too. According to the Talmud, "he who weds his daughter to an old man, and he who gives a wife unto his minor son, commits a wrong."[9] The Torah, as you probably already know, directs that if a man dies without a child, his brother is obliged to marry the widow and to give her a child to carry on the dead man's name. Chapter twenty-five of Deuteronomy, verses five through ten, describe the procedure to be followed. We read that if a man is reluctant to fulfill this obligation, "the elders of his city shall call him and speak to him." In commenting on this passage, the Talmud says:

> This teaches that they gave him advice suitable for him. If he was young and she old, or vice versa, they would say to him, "What sense is there in your marrying one much younger than yourself?" or "What sense is there in your marrying one much older than yourself? Go, marry one who is about your own age and do not introduce strife into your house."

In addition to the unconscious motivations involved, there are two very important practical problems to be considered when the bride is very much younger than the groom. The life expectancy of women in the United States is considerably longer than that of men. This means that even when husband and wife are of approximately the same age, the man is likely to die first and the woman will face a certain number of years toward the end of her life as a widow. Where an age disparity exists, with the husband much older than his wife, this probability is obviously increased. While this is not a very pleasant or happy prospect to consider at the time of one's choice of a marriage partner, long-range possibilities must be faced in making a decision one hopes will last for life.

The other practical difficulty pertains to the future sex life of the couple. There is no reason for a woman twenty and a man thirty-five to face any trouble in this regard. When she is fifty, however, and he sixty-five, serious problems of sexual adjustment may develop.

9. *Interest in other people* is also an area where compatibility is to be tested. As with attitudes toward the saving or spending of money, the kind of people one likes indicates much about one's own personality. Everything else being equal, two people who like each other's friends, who react similarly to a third person whom they have both met for the first time, are likely to face a brighter

IS THIS A GOOD MATCH?

future together than two who normally disagree about other people. It is worth observing here that individuals who have many friends of their own sex usually make better marriages than those with few friends.

10. *It would be difficult to exaggerate the importance of religious compatibility.* This includes not only the advantage of bride and groom coming from the same general religious faith, but also the attitudes of the two toward religious belief and practice even when they share a common religious background. Since we intend to comment on this at greater length later, it is merely mentioned here briefly as one of the important areas of life in which compatibility is essential.

11. It would not surprise us at all to hear a howl of dissension when we mention *compatibility between the two families involved in a prospective match.* We can almost hear many of our readers protesting with vehemence: "But I'm not marrying a family! I'm marrying an individual, and that's all that counts!"

True, one marries an individual. But it would be a disastrous error to assume that the family of the individual can therefore be ignored. Most young couples live in the same community with the parents of one or both of the partners. Unless they can get along well together, there is trouble lurking in the not-too-distant future. A wife whose husband is at odds with her parents becomes the rope in an emotional tug-of-war. A husband whose wife is at war with his parents is in no less lamentable a position. Many a marriage has floundered catastrophically on the rocks of in-law trouble. The writer of this book has discovered, in many years of counseling engaged and married couples, that the in-law problem is the one most frequently raised as a barrier to happiness. While it is undeniably true that sometimes this is just a convenient distraction to camouflage serious deficiencies on the part of husband or wife, the fact remains that one is wise to give the most serious kind of thought to the family of one's intended.

Aside from everything else, the family of your mate will be important in determining the heredity of your children. Remember that half your children's chromosomes and genes will come from your family, the other half from the family of your mate. It is entirely possible that some trait—physical or emotional—which you find extremely objectionable in your future father-in-law or mother-in-law may show up conspicuously in your own child.

Our tradition scores high in recognizing the importance of this factor too. The Talmud enjoins: "Before taking a wife, investigate her brothers, for most children resemble their mother's brothers."[10]

> Is it true genetically that most children resemble their maternal uncles? If so, what would this mean for us in anticipating our prospects for marital happiness? If this is not true, would it justify our forgetting the talmudic injunction altogether? Why?

Transferring the major love relationship of grown children from their parents to their mates is sometimes a painful problem. It is not easy for parents to let go, to stop after so many years of directing their children's lives and to accept them as mature adults. On the other hand, there are young people who have become too closely attached to one or both parents, and fail to make the necessary adjustment toward husband or wife as the most important recipient of love in their lives. In either event, the result can be disastrous.

Jewish tradition has long recognized the nature of this problem. Immediately after the Bible tells of Eve's being created as Adam's partner in life, it adds: "Therefore shall a man leave his father and mother, and shall cleave unto his wife, and they shall be one flesh." One of the post-biblical rabbis added: "Before a man marries, his love goes to his parents; after he marries, his love goes to his wife."[11]

> Do you agree with the statement made by this rabbi? What was he trying to say? Could he have said it better?

In this connection, there is also the question of whether a young married couple should live in the household of either parent. Jewish tradition has a number of things to say about this. The Talmud, for example, asks: "Can a goat live in the same barn as a tiger? In the same fashion, a daughter-in-law cannot live with her mother-in-law under the same roof." Without inquiring too specifically into which of the two is to be identified with the goat and which the tiger, the point our rabbis meant to emphasize is clear.

Two very interesting comments on this matter come from the Apocrypha. In your judgment, are they consistent or in disagreement? The first goes: "I have carried iron and removed stones, and they were not heavier than for a man to settle in his father-in-law's house." The other reads: "Honor your father-in-law and mother-in-law, because henceforth they are your parents."[12]

Recognizing the need for practical guidance in facing the problem of in-laws, the *Shulchan Aruch* stipulates that if either husband or wife finds the visits of parents-in-law or other relatives disturbing to the peace of the household, such visits are to be prohibited. Neither mate, however, can deny the other the right to visit his or her parents in their home.[13]

> Is this sound advice? Is a happy marriage possible where either partner insists that the other may visit his parents in their home but not invite them as guests?

12. Though we begin this section by stating that incompatibility does not always mean sexual uncongeniality, there is no denying that it sometimes does. Sex is very important in marriage—so important that we plan shortly to devote several chapters to it. For that reason, we merely list here *the need for sexual compatibility,* deferring our discussion to a later section.

In General

Several summary comments are needed here on the general subject of compatibility. First, it would be foolish to suppose that any two people can or should be identical in all respects. Indeed, their household would likely be a dull and boring place if this were so. What is important is not that bride and groom be carbon copies of one another, but that they resemble each other in most respects and do not differ too widely in the rest.

It is a dreadful mistake to marry someone with whom one knows he is seriously incompatible, in the expectation that after marriage he will change his mate. True, two people who live lovingly in a good marriage do have an effect on each other; it has been said that sometimes husbands and wives come not only to think alike but almost seem to resemble each other. But this is true only if there was sufficient compatibility to begin with. A home is not a reform school. If you don't love your prospective mate as he or she is, quit before you become too deeply involved!

Professor F. Alexander Magoun, whom we have quoted earlier in these pages, has made a wise and eloquent comment on this subject:

> The only person one ever has the right to try to change is one's self. Immaturity often manifests itself in an attempt to reform the betrothed. A mature person sees faults, balances them against virtues, and accepts another individual for what he is.[14]

Incidentally, beware, if you find no faults in your intended! There never has been and never will be a perfect human being. If you can identify no faults, it means you don't know the other person anywhere near as well as you think you do. You may be sure of one thing: sooner or later after the wedding, faults will become evident—in you and in your mate. To know them in advance means to be prepared for the adjustments you will later have to make. There is another reason it is important to recognize faults in the person you intend to marry. To love means to fulfill the needs of the loved one. If you are unaware of that person's faults, how can you possibly know—far less, fulfill—his needs?

It is essential that you like your mate as well as love him. Actually, we are begging the question in this statement, because if you do not truly like and respect him, it isn't love at all but at best, only infatuation. A good question to ask is whether the person you think you might want to marry is one whom you would find interesting, with whom you would want to spend a great deal of time, from whose companionship you could learn and grow, even if there were no sexual attraction involved. This is not an easy question to answer, but it is an essential one to ask.

Other people with whom we become emotionally involved can have a variety of effects on us. They can make us feel—
    a. Inferior, or
    b. Superior, flattered, possessing an inflated ego, or
    c. Satisfied with ourselves as we are, or
    d. Acceptable to ourselves as we are but eager to improve.
Neither the first nor the second kind of reaction is a promising one for marriage. The third is acceptable; only the fourth is really good.

Some years ago, the writer visited an elderly man who had lost his wife the day before. They had been married more than fifty years. As the old man talked to his rabbi, he kept nodding his head sadly from side to side, saying: "Did I lose a friend! I lost the most wonderful friend a man could have!" He came eloquently and pathetically close to summarizing what we are trying to convey here. If, in addition to everything else which binds them together, a man and woman can feel they are solid friends to each other, theirs is apt to be a superb marriage.

The Talmud contains the following rather curious statement: "Every man receives the wife he deserves."[15]

How To Make the Right Choice   81

Do you agree? If so, why? If not, is there some element of truth in this assertion?

On Reaching a Decision

A number of tests have been devised to evaluate the personalities of two individuals who are contemplating marriage and to anticipate their probable compatibility. While no such test is infallible, and life's most important decisions cannot be made entirely on the basis of psychological tests, such tests can nevertheless be helpful, particularly where there is reason to doubt how well any two people are matched. Most rabbis and marriage counselors are aware of these tests and can arrange to administer them to couples who want to know more about themselves, both individually and together.

Since it is likely to be several years until most of you will be ready for this kind of intensive test, we offer you here a brief chart with which two people may attempt to evaluate themselves and the relationship between them. It is adapted by the author from a similar chart originally published in Crawford and Woodward's book, *Better Ways of Growing Up,* published by the Muhlenberg Press. To be justified in considering themselves compatible, any two individuals should be much alike on at least half these items, somewhat alike on many of the rest, and without major discrepancies on more than four or five.

For Instance

A. Bob is one of the most intelligent young men in his college class. He was elected to the National Honor Society in high school and became a member of Phi Beta Kappa in his junior year at the university. He loves people, is warm and outgoing in personality, makes friends easily, and quickly becomes the center of conversation in any crowd. Laura is quite the opposite. While not stupid by any means, she had to work very hard in both high school and college; one year she had to attend summer session to make up a course she had flunked. She did manage to graduate with slightly

HOW COMPATIBLE ARE WE?

1. VERY DIFFERENT

2. MILDLY DIFFERENT

3. SOMEWHAT ALIKE

4. MUCH ALIKE

TRAITS	RATINGS
1. Home Background	
2. Personal standards of right and wrong	
3. Ideals regarding home and family	
4. Desires for and feelings toward children	
5. Educational background and interests	
6. Intelligence	
7. Religious interests and preferences	
8. Vocational preferences and attitudes	
9. Ambition for money and social standing	
10. Spending and saving habits	
11. Relative emphasis on home and outside activities	
12. Cultural tastes: art, music, drama, books, etc.	
13. Personal habits: eating, sleeping, smoking, etc.	
14. Circle of friends	
15. Recreational and social interests	
16. Temperament and mood	
17. Punctuality and neatness	
18. Attitudes toward parents of both	
19. Tendency to be critical	
20. Tendency to praise and reassure	

How To Make the Right Choice 83

lower than average grades. Socially she is shy and retiring, generally uncomfortable in the presence of people she has met for the first time. In a gathering she likes to sit back and listen to others, rarely offering to contribute anything herself.

Bob and Laura are aware of these differences between them but feel that, far from being liabilities, they enhance their relationship. Laura glows with pride whenever she listens to Bob holding forth on any subject. He, on his part, seems to want and need the adulation she gives him. "We complement each other perfectly," they have often said. "Each of us supplies what the other needs."

> What do you think this couple's chances are for a happy and successful marriage? Are they likely to feel this way permanently about the differences between them? Why?

B. Harry thinks Phyllis is a spendthrift; this is the most serious fault he can find in her. He himself has come from an impoverished family and has had to work hard for everything he possesses. With diligent work and careful savings, he has built up a comfortable amount of reserves and is very careful about how he spends his money. He attributes the fact that Phyllis doesn't know the value of a dollar to the wealth of her parents, who have always given her everything she ever wanted.

They have discussed this difference a number of times and think they can overcome it. Harry has made it clear that he will marry Phyllis only on condition that he is to be the manager of all their financial matters. He will give Phyllis an allowance, reviewing it with her from time to time, but the final decisions are to be his. This is the only area in which he insists on being the boss. Phyllis is willing to accept such an arrangement because she is confident her parents will continue to give her whatever she may want which she will be unable to purchase from her allowance.

It should be added that Harry is also much neater than Phyllis. He is willing, however, to let her keep the house in the way she wishes, so long as he can be in charge of his own closets and dresser.

> How important is it that Phyllis and Harry have faced this problem and arrived at a solution? Do you foresee any

great difficulty between them after they are married? Should Phyllis tell Harry of her expectations from her family or leave well enough alone in order not to create unnecessary pre-marital disagreement?

C. When Alvin comes home in the evening from a hard day's work he wants nothing so much as to sit down after dinner at the television set and spend a relaxed few hours watching. Brenda doesn't care much for television; an hour or two on Sunday is enough for her. She is, however, extremely fond of bridge, finding it the most relaxing diversion she knows. They have agreed that Alvin will watch television as often and as long as he likes, while she is to feel free to join three of her bridge-playing girl friends. They have, as a matter of fact, followed this kind of schedule several nights a week throughout their engagement and it seems to have worked out well. The only serious disagreements between them have taken place on Sunday afternoons when they have from time to time watched TV together. Then Alvin invariably wants to see a football or baseball game and Brenda, who doesn't care for athletics at all, would prefer an entertainment program. They have had a few unpleasant arguments over this but aren't particularly worried because they plan to have two television sets after their marriage so each can watch what he wants.

> How successful do you think this marriage will be? Are Alvin and Brenda likely to have other problems of disagreement? Do you think their arrangements will be as successful in married life as they seem to have been during their engagement? Why?

D. What do you think is the point of the following rabbinic story? "Three years had passed since the day Abraham had sent Ishmael away. He longed to see him, and sought out his camp in the pasture-country of Paran. When Abraham came to his son's tent, he found Ishmael absent from home. He asked Ishmael's wife for a little water, but the ill-natured woman refused to give it to him. Abraham said: 'When thy husband returns, pray tell him that an old man from Philistia came to visit him, and not finding him home, offered this advice: the pegs of your tent should be changed.'

"Ishmael understood this allusion to his wicked wife and divorced her. He wedded another woman, named Fatima.

"The following year Abraham again wished to visit his son and again found him away from home. Without waiting for a request, Fatima offered him hospitality, and urged him to partake of food and drink. Abraham said: 'When thy husband returns, tell him: his pegs are excellent and he should retain them.'

"Ishmael thanked his gracious wife, and blessed the Lord who had sent him so admirable a mate."[16]

> Did Abraham have the right to interfere in this way in his married son's life? Was he entirely fair to Ishmael's first wife? What do you think is the point of this story? In the light of what had occurred earlier in the life of Abraham and Ishmael (see Genesis 16:1–16 and 21:1–21), is any light shed on the failure of the young man's first marriage? In view of past events, is there anything surprising in the outcome of the story?

E. Hilda's mother is angry and bitter. She feels that her son-in-law, Irving, has poisoned her daughter's mind against her own parents. Before Hilda's marriage, she and her parents had been very close. At first Hilda phoned her mother every day and consulted with her frequently over recipes and other household matters. Then Irving began to interfere. He resented the amount of time his wife was spending with her mother and the fact that she was still so dependent on her. Where once the couple would visit Hilda's parents every Sunday, Irving now insists that they visit his parents as often as hers and that they should spend some Sundays away from all four parents. Hilda tells her mother that she agrees with her but her husband is so unreasonable on this subject that she doesn't dare risk an open break with him. Things have reached the point now where her mother feels most uncomfortable when the four of them are together. She and Irving barely acknowledge each other. The atmosphere is almost like one of armed neutrality.

> Judging by the facts presented here, where does the fault lie for this sad situation? Is Hilda's mother being reasonable? Is Irving? Has Hilda handled the problem wisely? What could be done to improve matters? Could Hilda's

father do anything to help? If things go on as they thus far have, do you think Hilda and Irving will be drawn closer together?

F. As far back as Claire can remember, her father has been "master" of their house. All important decisions are made by him. Neither her mother, her sister, nor she herself would think of taking a major step without seeking and following his advice. True, there were occasions, especially during her early adolescent years, when she resented her father's authority, but he has been wise in his decisions for the family and she likes the idea of a strong man on whom she can depend.

Quite the opposite has been true in Vic's family. His father is a kind, soft-spoken man who has never been decisive. Each week he hands his paycheck to his wife, who proceeds to pay the bills and manage the family's funds. She has been a rock to all of them, keeping calm under stress, resolving every indecision for her husband and children. While Vic's sister has often bitterly resented her mother's strength, he has enormous respect for that strength and has learned to rely on it in every crisis.

Claire and Vic have just announced their engagement. They and their families are excited in anticipation of the wedding, which has been scheduled for next summer.

If you were a rabbi or marriage counselor, what advice would you give Claire and Vic? Why? Do you foresee any particular problems in their marriage? Could you—by pointing out such problems to them—eliminate them as dangers to the couple's happiness?

Chapter SEVEN

RECIPE FOR SUCCESS

BY NOW WE KNOW THAT THE FIRST INGREDIENT OF A HAPPY MAR-
riage is a wise choice of mate. This, however, is only a beginning.
Even two people who are compatible in most respects can fail if
they do not attend to the rules best calculated to bring them
closer together through the years. The relationship between husband and wife is so intimate that it cannot be a static one. In
some ways it may be compared to an airplane which must keep
moving forward or fall to the ground. So most couples discover
that they either move closer together or farther apart during
their years of marriage.

Strange as it may sound, love and hate are very closely related
emotions. Infants are born with a nearly insatiable need for love;
there is no such thing as an inborn need to hate. Someone has
defined hate as love gone sour. When a little child fails to receive

the kind and amount of love he requires, especially from his parents, his innate capacity to give love can turn into a need to hate. Much the same process can occur in a marriage. The need of most adults for one partner in life—to whom they can give and from whom they can receive the most profound kind of love a human being is capable of knowing—is so deep that if it becomes frustrated, the probable consequence is hate. It is always sad to see a husband and wife, who began their life together with such high hopes for continuing love, reach the point of hating each other. But it sometimes happens.

Standing at the marriage altar, almost all couples are confident that they face a happy and loving future. The statistics of divorce show that too many of them are disappointed. In the United States, between 1870 and 1940, while the population was increasing threefold and the number of marriages fourfold, the number of divorces rose twentyfold!

It is important to remember two things in considering these statistics. First, not every unsuccessful marriage reaches the point of divorce. Numbers of unhappy couples remain together for a variety of reasons. To borrow the wonderful phrase of Thoreau, they remain under one roof, living together their "lives of quiet desperation." On the other hand, however, it would be a mistake to assume that the entire increase in divorce represents that much additional unhappiness.

The attitude of our society toward divorce has also changed substantially since 1870. There was a time when divorce was considered a scandal and a divorced person was looked at askance. Fortunately, this is no longer so. Because divorce is now socially more acceptable than it once was, there is little doubt that a higher proportion of unhappy couples resort to it than they did in the past. In whatever way we qualify or interpret these statistics, however, the fact remains that too many couples fail in their efforts to achieve a happy marriage.

We have earlier referred to the fact that in marriage, as in life generally, happiness does not come to us automatically. It results only from understanding the laws of human nature and striving to conform to those laws. Too often couples concentrate only on the benefits they hope to receive from marriage, ignoring the means through which these benefits are possible. Given two individuals who are at least reasonably well matched, what are some of the factors which experience and study have shown to be instrumental in the making of a good marriage?

One is the amount of kindness and consideration each partner in the marriage shows to the other. One of the saddest spectacles in life is the thoughtful attention so many couples show during their courtship and engagement, contrasted to the manner in which they take each other for granted afterward. A Stradivarius violin, abandoned to accumulate dirt and dust, soon loses its purity of tone. A love relationship, taken for granted and neglected, becomes tarnished and marred. No marriage can survive indifference.

Because Jewish tradition understood this, it adjured husband and wife always to show by their behavior how much they loved each other. In an earlier context we quoted the Zohar as saying: "A wife who receives love gives love in return; if she receives anger, she returns anger in equal measure." A Midrash is more explicit on the same point:

> A wise woman said to her daughter, who was about to become a bride: "My daughter, if you will respect your husband like a king, he will treat you like a queen. If you will serve him like a slavegirl, he will serve you like a slave. But if you will be too proud to serve him, he will assert his mastership by force and will treat you like a maid-servant. If your husband is about to visit his friends, persuade him to bathe and wear fine raiment. If his friends come to his house, welcome them heartily and set before them more than they can eat, so that they will respect your husband. Watch well your home and all of your husband's possessions. He will be delighted with you, and you will be the crown of his head."[1]

> Would you accept this as sound advice for the modern couple? Are there any corrections or improvements you would suggest in it? Does it contain anything which could conceivably do more harm than good in a marriage?

Root of All Evil

Another factor on which the success of a marriage hinges is the ability of the couple to cooperate in handling their financial affairs. True, a failure here often simply reflects a deeper problem, but the fact remains that the economics of marriage must be successfully managed.

How much money two people need depends on their values, their ambitions, and the standard of living they hope to achieve. One thing which is certain is that wealth by itself is no guarantee of success. One marriage counselor has reported an interesting study he made in the area of Los Angeles. In an exclusive suburb, he met a family whose income was $100,000 a year but whose home was filled with bickering, worry, and angry conflict. In a trailer court, he spoke to a crippled man who lived with his arthritic wife and adolescent daughter. They were supremely happy on the very small income he earned as a part-time watchman. These two couples scored lowest and highest respectively of all families studied in Los Angeles County on a marriage adjustment test given by the counselor.[2] This does not mean that all wealthy couples are unhappy and all families of low income are happy. Financial tension is often a problem which jeopardizes the success of a marriage. It is desirable for each couple to have at least a decent minimum of economic security. But money alone will never assure the success of a marriage.

The author remembers counseling an attractive young couple who were experiencing difficulty during the first year of their marriage. Near the end of an hour's discussion he said to them: "One of your troubles is that you have financial problems." They were startled and protested with vehemence. "Oh no," they both insisted, "that's one area where we have no worries at all. We have both inherited quite a bit of money and stock from our grandparents and can have just about everything we want." This the author had known. He proceeded to explain that it is possible to have financial problems because of too much which comes too easily, as well as because of too little.

What helps most in this regard is for husband and wife to have similar economic expectations and desires and to be able to plan and implement their budget together. If both were in the habit of living by carefully planned budgets while single, they have an initial advantage.

A wife whose demands exceed her husband's ability to provide can put severe strain on their partnership. The rabbis were aware of this too. They incorporated the following in the Midrash:

> Once a man engaged in robbery by night, keeping his family in luxury as a consequence. The wife of a neighbor complained to her husband: "What ill-luck is mine that I am married to you. The man across the way keeps his family in every comfort." The husband replied: "But rumor has it that he is a thief. Do you wish me to become like him?" The wife answered: "I care not what your occupation is, provided you give me the luxuries I crave." Being enamored of his wife, the husband begged his neighbor to allow him to participate in his next enterprise. The police were informed and laid a trap for him. The experienced robber succeeded in escaping the snare but the novice was captured and hanged.[3]

Many husbands, in our day too, are impelled to indulge in questionable business practices by the excessive demands of their wives and sometimes, their children. For this reason it is wise for husbands to share with their wives, as much as possible, their general financial condition—what they can afford without undue strain, how much is being set aside for insurance, emergency and retirement, what it is realistic to expect their income to be in the future.

How about working wives? A generation or two ago most husbands would probably have considered it a reflection on their own manliness and ability to have their wives help in the support of the household. Today a substantial proportion of wives, particularly during the early years of marriage, continue to work. If the husband is opposed for the reason just described, or the wife resents her need to supplement their income, this can be a serious problem. If both are mature, a working wife can add more to the marriage than just extra income. There are so many electric housekeeping devices available today that most young wives need only a small fraction of their time to clean and maintain their homes.

A woman who occupies herself with gratifying and meaningful activity, who feels needed and useful as a person, will probably be a better wife to her husband and one day, a better mother to her children as a result. The important thing here is not just how much she earns, or indeed, whether she earns anything at all. If there is no need for supplementation to the husband's income, a volunteer job can accomplish as much, provided it offers work which the wife really feels to be important and which gives her a sense of fulfilling herself.

Planning Ahead

There is another reason why many marriage counselors now advise young wives to work, at least until children begin to arrive, and to resume work, perhaps on a part-time schedule, when their full attention is no longer needed by the family. At the age of menopause or change-of-life, which comes to most women some time between the ages of 45 and 55, there are often emotional difficulties which can be disturbing. Aside from certain glandular changes which occur in a woman's body at this time of life, a complicating factor is that her husband is still at the peak of his business or professional career, her children are away at college or perhaps already married themselves—and suddenly she becomes aware of the fact that from 8 A.M. to 6 P.M. there is no one in the world who really needs her, no position of importance and usefulness for her to fill. The woman who has kept her hand on a career may be better able to cope with this period of her life than one who has done nothing but attend the needs of her family.

Is it possible for a wife to follow this advice without neglecting her family responsibilities? The answer to this must depend largely on the individual; among other things, how much energy and ambition she possesses. Certain studies undertaken at Columbia University seem to indicate that working wives may actually spend more meaningful time with their children than wives who do not work.[4] The important thing is not so much the number of minutes or hours spent in the home by women and their children, but rather what they do with the time spent together. Surely a woman's responsibilities to her family must come first. If she seeks a job outside her home as an escape from these duties, her marriage is bound to suffer. If she can fulfill both types of obligation without ignoring or neglecting her home, this is good.

Two statements in the Talmud appear to be contradictory on this point. The first, which we have already cited in another context, reads: "He who looks for the earnings of his wife sees never a sign of blessing." The second: "It is not seemly for a woman to sit in idleness."[5]

> Do these two statements refer to the same thing? Can they be reconciled? How do you suppose the rabbis in talmudic times would have felt about working wives? How appropriate would their attitudes on this be for us today? Why?

Before we leave the problems of money in marriage, you may be interested in knowing that certain male occupations seem to carry with them a somewhat higher probability of happy marriages than do others. Among these are professors, chemical engineers, and the clergy. Occupations showing a lower degree of success in marriage are laborers, mechanics, and traveling salesmen.

How significant do you think this conclusion is? Should it deter a girl from seriously considering marriage to a man in any of the last-named occupations? Why? Can we account for the differences because of the occupations themselves or because of the types of individuals who would be attracted by them?

A Fringe Is Not Enough

Another factor of great consequence in determining the success of a particular marriage is the amount of time the two partners (and ultimately their children) spend together in meaningful ways. The relative ease with which household chores may now be performed, the incessant demands a man's business or profession often make on his time, the shrieking distractions which tempt us both within and outside our homes—these are characteristics of contemporary life which have in some instances corroded the true partnership of marriage.

In Chapter Six we observed that an important prerequisite for the wise choice of a mate is the capacity of two individuals to share life. This capacity is of little value, however, unless they actually *do* share it. Far too frequently, after the first excitement and flush of the honeymoon have subsided, husband and wife go their separate ways, sharing a roof and a bed, but not truly sharing the most significant aspects of their lives. The writer recalls an occasion some years back when he sat with a shocked and stunned husband whose wife had died that very day. They had been married over thirty years. Yet, when the bereaved husband was asked what his wife's interests were outside her family, and who her closest friends were, the man, after a minute or two of troubled thought, confessed: "Rabbi, I just can't answer that question . . . I don't know." In that pathetic reply he conveyed to his rabbi far more than he had really intended.

We have just referred in passing to the almost irresistible distractions which have made inroads in our family life. There was a time when families did many things together, sometimes things which were essential to the family economy, and sometimes things planned simply for fun. The important thing is that they were done together; often it became impossible even to distinguish the job from the diversion. Today there is almost nothing the members of a family must do together to keep the family going, and in most of the things we do together for recreation, we have become passive spectators, who just happen to be doing things in the same place and the same time, but not really together. A study made in the state of California, even before the wholesale advent of television, showed that 76.4 per cent of total leisure time activity there was spent passively watching others do something, rather than actively performing oneself. With television as popular as it now is, the figure would obviously be even higher. A family sitting together in one room watching a TV program (that is, assuming they are not in several rooms, each watching his own favorite program on his own set) is of course preferable to a family scattered to the four winds, but such a family is not forging unbreakable bonds of unity and love among its members.

Dr. James A. Peterson has expressed this thought with exceptional eloquence:

> Hard physical effort such as scaling a mountain or hiking a great distance or lugging a canoe over a portage or playing a hard fought set of tennis—all of these enable us to release some of the aggressions built up within us. We invest ourselves in these activities and when they are finished there has taken place a kind of catharsis that has value.
>
> There is a type of psychological help for children called play therapy which is based on the definite recognition that creative play enables the child to release feelings hitherto inhibited. In the same way the play of husband and wife releases pent-up feelings and clears the way for more positive feelings.
>
> Recreational events are the sunshine among shadows, the highlights of sometimes gray marital experience. But every experience in the family in-

fluences all other experiences. When a couple solves
their difficulties in a game they are provided with a
new pattern for solving difficulties in other areas.
After several such recreational experiences the
budget-planning session will be conducted in a
little different atmosphere with more gaiety and
good humor.[6]

It is unfortunate that so many husbands and wives live the recreational aspects of their lives almost entirely apart from each other.
They play tennis or golf or cards with friends of the same sex, and
are sometimes separated at social gatherings, even for the purpose
of after-dinner conversation. During much of the week and year
the dictates of economic and communal necessity leave them little
choice. But how often—on weekends and at times of leisure—do
they rush away from each other, almost as if they feared to learn
more about each other! The husband or wife who puts his marriage out on the fringes of experience, giving it only the crumbs of
his attention and time, cannot expect much happiness or satisfaction. The members of a family who use their home as a motel—a
convenient place to sleep, change clothes and eat—occasionally but
not necessarily performing some of these functions together—cannot hope to realize the rich promise of either marriage or love.

Also Important

Brief mention must be made of several other factors which affect the success of a marriage. One is the love relationship which bride and groom have seen between their own respective parents. In ways which are deeply significant, even though mostly on an unconscious level, what children hear and see transpiring between their mothers and fathers makes a permanent imprint on their own lives. It affects their stability and maturity; it offers them a paradigm of what marriage should be. Some years ago Dr. Paul Popenoe completed an interesting study of the relationship between the happiness of married couples and that of the homes from which they came. Over 4,000 couples were involved. Of those who grew up in happy homes, 67 per cent had achieved happiness in their own marriages. Of those who had emerged from unhappy homes, only 43 per cent were happy themselves. This is worth pondering.

It does not mean, however, that if your parents were unhappy and their marriage was unsuccessful, you are thereby doomed to repeat the pattern yourself. In that event, the wise thing for you to do is to find out, if you can, what went wrong in *their* marriage. Why did they fail to fulfill the expectations they harbored on their wedding day? What was there—about themselves as individuals, about their maturity or lack of it, about their understanding of marriage—which derailed them? In short, if your parents were inadequate for marriage or made mistakes, you can learn and even benefit from their mistakes.

Religion plays a large role, too, in determining the success of a marriage. It will interest you to know that couples whose weddings take place in a synagogue or church show a significantly higher probability of happiness than those whose ceremonies are conducted elsewhere. This is not due to any special magic emanating from sanctuaries, but to the fact that the kind of person to whom religion and a religious setting for his wedding would be important is also apt to be the kind of person whose values and maturity qualify him for happiness in marriage. We say no more at this point about religion as a factor making for marital success, because a later chapter will be entirely devoted to this very topic.

You may have begun to wonder why, in discussing the determinants of happiness in marriage, no mention has yet been made of a good sexual relationship. Our reason has been the conviction that a good sex adjustment is more likely to be the consequence than the cause of a good marriage. In any event, our next several chapters will be devoted to various aspects of sex, so we shall defer further consideration of this very important topic for the moment. First, however, there is a final consideration which calls for our attention in this chapter.

Courtship and Engagement

All studies show that the length and kind of engagement experienced by a couple has something to do with the quality of their marriage. At the beginning of this book, when we first tried to distinguish between love and infatuation, we observed that a lasting quality is an important characteristic of love. The proper kind of engagement gives each couple a chance to use the test of time. It affords them an opportunity to know each other better and test their relationship. No one can prescribe the length of time an engagement should last. While it would appear from various investigations that a period of at least a year is best, this varies from couple to couple. What two people do during their engagement, how they use their time of testing, is more important than the actual length of their engagement. Two people who have known each other well for a long time before they become engaged will obviously not need as long a period of engagement as will two who have met recently.

It would be unwise, however, to underestimate the desirability of an engagement which is long enough to perform its proper functions. It is easy for a couple who have known each other for only a few months to say: "Yes, but we have been together almost every evening during that time and have become far more knowledgeable of each other than many couples who have known each other longer." One hundred hours spent together over a period of a few weeks is nowhere near as good a barometer of compatibility as the same number spread over a longer span of time. Months of close contact provide a better opportunity than weeks, and a year is a better index than a few months in judging the probability of success for any given couple.

Nothing is more important during courtship and engagement than utter honesty between prospective bride and groom. There is a danger that they may come to know only the best side of each other before marriage. One purpose of the engagement, therefore, should be to see each other under adverse as well as favorable conditions; to discover how they react to a variety of circumstances, how they handle themselves when they are frustrated and disappointed and grouchy as well as when they are on a high tide of satisfaction. It is desirable also for each to see how the other acts in his own family setting and to become acquainted with his future in-laws.

The engagement should also be a time for planning the future. In addition to plans for the wedding, the prospective bride and groom should discuss where they are to live, whether in rented quarters or their own home, how many children they want to have and approximately when, the nature and intensity of their religious identification, whether or not the wife is to work, and their feelings toward each other's parents. Careful attention should be given also to their budget, including the proportion of their income to be assigned to insurance and savings. Two people who cannot amicably, intelligently, lovingly make such plans as these during their engagement had better think searchingly about the advisability of marrying.

The sexual relationship between a man and woman during their engagement is of obvious importance too. This will be discussed in a later chapter, after we shall have considered the role of sex in marriage.

In Summary

We have by no means exhausted all the considerations on which the happiness of a married couple depends. Our hope has been to call your attention to the most important of them and to stimulate your own thinking. How happy your marriage will be depends not only on how wisely you choose your wife or husband, but also on the intelligence and care with which the two of you pay attention to the conditions discussed in these past few pages. Among the factors which determine the success of a marriage are the following: the kindness and consideration which husband and wife give each other . . . the degree of agreement between them on money matters . . . the ability of the wife to fulfill herself through purposeful activity . . . the amount of time they spend together, especially in creative directions . . . the love relationship which bride and groom saw between their parents . . . the quality of their religious life . . . the satisfactions derived through their sex life . . . the extent to which they have wisely used their period of engagement to learn more about each other and to plan their future.

For Instance

A. Terry had noticed how irritable Sam had been in the recent past but had no idea of the cause. Whenever she questioned him about his health, he brushed her queries aside and changed the subject. Since she found that further probing only increased his testiness, she soon stopped asking. The real reason for all this was that Sam had been facing serious business reverses. Several deals on which he had counted had fallen through and payments due him were late in arriving.

Sam was worried but did not want to involve his wife in matters which were his own responsibility. Applications to send both children to camp had already gone in and a mink coat Terry had wanted for years had been ordered. It wouldn't be fair, Sam thought, to deprive the kids of camp or to disappoint Terry who had been so excited over the coat. The chest pains he had experienced over the past few days he attributed to the strain and worry; he was confident that as soon as things eased up a little in business he would feel much better. Meanwhile Terry found that she was responding to Sam's irritability in kind, so that the atmosphere in their home had been deteriorating.

What do you think of Sam's thoughtfulness toward his wife and children? What did it show about Sam himself? About his marriage? Should Terry have been more insistent in ascertaining the cause of her husband's irritability?

B. Read the story of Abraham's way of finding a wife for his son Isaac. You will find it in Genesis 24:1–27. Then be prepared to discuss the following questions, based on this story:

What criteria did Abraham give his servant for selecting Isaac's bride? What criteria did the servant establish for himself? Were they wise? Did Rebecca meet them? Are there any other qualities described in this passage which would suggest Rebecca's desirability as a wife? Can we learn anything here which is applicable to the subject of this chapter?

C. Al has never worked so hard in his life. A few years ago he quit the job he had held for ten years, and together with an old friend, started a business of his own. The two partners both invested every dollar they had saved in this new business, plus a considerable amount of money they had borrowed.

For five years now, since their firm was founded, both partners have given it practically every hour of their waking time. Al is at the office daily by seven A.M. and seldom leaves before seven P.M. On Sundays he allows himself the luxury of sleeping until eight, but after breakfast drops by the plant "for a couple of hours." More often than not, it is dinner time Sunday evening before he returns home.

Sue has complained about the almost total absence of her husband from their home. She feels it isn't fair either to her or their three children. Al is very understanding; he says he doesn't blame her for feeling this way but he just can't help himself. "Honey," he keeps saying, "I have no choice. I'm really doing this, you know, for you and the kids. It's your future security and theirs that I want to provide. Once we get this business off the ground I'll try to turn over some of my responsibilities to others and spend more time with the family. But for the time being, it will have to be this way." When Sue protests that "for the time being" has already lasted for five years, and asks how much longer it will be, Al can give no answer beyond assuring her he will do the best he can.

> How much obligation does a husband owe his family in terms of providing for their future financial security? In terms of being with them in the present? If the two are in conflict, which should take precedence? What is your guess as to how soon Al will find it possible to spend more time with Sue and his children? What does his conduct reveal about their marriage? What does it portend for its future?

D. Betty has been upset for the past three days, since Ralph suggested that they take their summer vacations separately. "During our engagement," she has reminded him, "you were annoyed with my parents because they wouldn't let me go with you on your vacation. Now we've been married only three years and already you don't want me with you. Here at home you spend practically all your time away from me because of business. When we have a chance to spend two weeks together, you don't want to."

Her arguments haven't made much impression on Ralph. "When we were engaged," he answered, "we were new to each other. Now that some of the novelty has worn off, let's act our age. You know I like to play golf on my vacation. I just don't enjoy playing golf with you; there's no competition. So let's go our separate ways for two weeks. I'll go some place where I can play golf with the boys, you go where you can swim, and as a result we'll probably love each other even more when we return home."

> Who is right in this argument? Why? Is it wrong for a married man to prefer playing golf with his male friends? Must husbands and wives do everything together? Would you call Betty a nagging wife?

Chapter EIGHT

SEX IS HERE TO STAY

YOU MAY BE INCLINED TO ASSUME THAT THIS WILL BE JUST ANOTHER routine recital of the so-called "facts of life," which you have heard many times and therefore do not need to hear again. It is true, of course, that some readers will need this chapter less than others, but we hope it will contain information of value for everyone. We have already seen that much of the "knowledge" of sex received even by intelligent young people must be placed in quotation marks because, coming from questionable sources, it is an unreliable—at times almost fantastic—combination of fact and fiction.

In order to test, at least partially, your own level of knowledge about sex, we give you here a list of fifteen terms which all of us must understand. Right now—before you proceed further with this chapter—write out for yourself one-sentence definitions of these words, numbering them as they are numbered below. Make your definitions as specific as you can. Keep the list; at the end of the chapter go over them again to see how well you scored. Here they are:

1. Vagina	6. Intercourse	11. Testicle
2. Womb	7. Petting	12. Scrotum
3. Celibate	8. Masturbation	13. Ovary
4. Virgin	9. Orgasm	14. Hymen
5. Penis	10. Coitus	15. Clitoris

Having done this, we are ready to consider the anatomy and physiology of sex in both males and females.

We are about to trace one of the most thrilling and exciting stories known to man. There is much evidence in the universe—in its orderliness and beauty, in the working together of so very many different elements and parts to serve important purposes—which convinces us that it could not be the result of mere happenstance or coincidence. The fact that scientists can learn enough about the laws of the universe, and can depend upon those laws to operate without deviation (and to permit us to fire a rocket toward the moon a quarter of a million miles away and have it land within about six miles of its target) is surely evidence enough for most of us that some kind of Intelligence or Power is responsible for everything that has ever existed. We call that Intelligence or Power God.

None of the evidence we find in outer space and on our own earth is more wonderfully convincing of this Intelligence than our own human bodies. The most highly skilled engineer using the most ingenious and complicated computer, could not possibly have planned bodies and minds which operate so efficiently and purposefully as ours do. The facts that, regardless of the temperature outside, the internal heat of the human body in normal health always remains within a fraction of a degree of what it should be . . . that no matter how much or how little liquid we drink, the proportion of water in our bodies is maintained at an even level . . . that when we ascend to higher altitudes where less oxygen is available, the red corpuscles in our blood immediately multiply in order to provide enough oxygen to keep us alive . . . that when infection strikes us, our white corpuscles mobilize at once to defend us . . . these and countless other manifestations of intelligence in the planning and operation of the human body impress us with the Intelligence which permeates the entire universe. (Incidentally, if you are interested in detailed descriptions of all this, you will find them in Chapter Three of the author's *Little Lower Than the Angels,* also published by the Union of American Hebrew Congregations.)

Nowhere, however, is this evidence more compellingly and beautifully illustrated than in the sex life of human beings. Millions of details in structure and function have been so designed that it is possible *through one act* for men and women to propagate their species (that is to say, produce offspring), to enjoy both physical and spiritual delight together, to express and simultaneously deepen their love, and to establish the foundation for families. In observing the truly amazing phenomena of human sex, you come perhaps as close as you ever will to following the way in which God operates in our lives. And some day, in experiencing all this with the man or woman you love, you will come closer than in any other way to God Himself.

How Sex Functions in Men

A diagram of the male sexual organs appears below. It shows first of all, the penis, which serves the double purpose of conveying from inside to outside the body, both urine from the bladder and a liquid substance called semen during sexual excitation. Here is one of the incredible feats of engineering we mentioned. The two functions of the penis could be so incompatible as to make one of them impossible. Urine contains a great deal of acid. Spermatozoa—the microscopic seeds needed to make a woman pregnant—cannot live in the presence of acid. If any acid from urine were to be in the urethra (the tube which extends inside the penis) when spermatozoa are flowing through it, they would immediately be killed and pregnancy could never occur. To prevent this, two things take place when a man becomes sexually excited. First, a muscle closes off the bladder, so that it becomes impossible for a man who is sexually aroused to urinate; second, the prostate gland produces an alkaline fluid which counteracts the effect of any acid which may have remained in the urethra from previous urination, thus making it possible for spermatozoa to remain alive. But we are a bit ahead of our story.

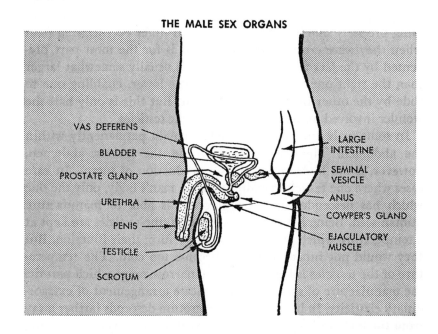

THE MALE SEX ORGANS

The size of the penis, like that of all other bodily parts, varies greatly from one person to the next. Normally, when a man is not sexually excited, the penis is in the limp position shown in the diagram and is likely to be about 3½ to 4 inches in length. When sexually aroused, it projects itself diagonally upward from the body, assuming a probable length of 5 to 6½ inches. There is no relationship between the size of the penis and the intensity of a man's sexual desires.

At birth, the tip of the penis is partially covered over with a flap of skin called the foreskin. Circumcision consists of removing this flap, so that the tip of the penis is fully exposed. In addition to the fact that it is a Jewish religious ritual symbolizing the covenant between God and Abraham, circumcision has been found to be healthy for the male and, for some reason which doctors do not yet fully understand, to reduce the probability of uterine cancer in the female.

Beneath the penis is a sack or bag called the scrotum, which contains the testicles. These are two small oval glands which manufacture spermatozoa (also called sperm). Again we discover magnificent planning. If his testicles were exactly the same size and hung precisely side by side, a man would suffer excruciating pain when they were crushed together. This is for the most part prevented by the fact that the left testicle is usually somewhat larger than the right one and hangs just a little lower, enabling one to slide by the other instead of crushing it. But this is only half the wonder involved in the arrangement of the testicles.

In some male animals the testicles remain permanently within the abdomen. The temperature within the human abdomen, however, is too high to permit the production of sperm. In rare cases where one testicle remains within a man's body, only the one which has descended into the scrotum is able to manufacture human seed. Being housed in the scrotum, the testicles are kept at a temperature which permits them to perform their function. But they would not function if they became too cold. The temperature of the testicles is kept within the narrow range which permits the manufacture of sperm by an intricate arrangement of extraordinary elasticity. In hot weather the scrotum descends farther away from the body to keep cool; in cold weather it contracts, bringing the testicles up closer to the body for warmth. See what we meant by the evidence of purpose and God in the way our bodies function? The most complicated thermostat invented by human intelligence cannot be more wondrous or dependable than this!

The testicles are not capable of producing sperm until a boy reaches the age of puberty, which usually occurs between the ages of ten and sixteen. The fact that in some boys it may come a little sooner or later than the average is of no significance at all in determining either the intensity or normality of their future sex life. As the testicles commence to perform their major function they also produce those physical changes which indicate that the boy is beginning to become a man: hair on his chest, surrounding his scrotum and appearing under his arms, a deepening of his voice, etc.

Once manufactured, the sperm are stored in the testicles and the vasa deferentia. When the supply exceeds the storage capacity, they are automatically released in the form of nocturnal emissions or, as they are more commonly called, "wet dreams." A boy who awakens in the morning to discover that during the night a quantity of liquid was apparently ejected from his penis, perhaps leaving stains on his pajamas and sheet, need not worry; this is nature's perfectly normal way of making room for the storage of more sperm. Often these emissions are accompanied by dreams which are sexually exciting. These too are perfectly normal; they should be the cause of neither fear nor guilt.

Each vas deferens has a seminal vesicle attached to it, the function of which is to supply a yellowish substance which makes the semen thicker, hence better able to carry and preserve the sperm. Ordinarily the seminal vesicles are kept closed by muscles in the prostate gland; it is only during sexual excitement that they open, permitting the secretion to pass into the urethra and become part of the semen.

Finally, there is Cowper's gland—named after the doctor who first discovered it. This gland secretes a slippery fluid which serves the same purpose in sexual intercourse that lubricating oil does in the engine of a car. The upward-downward motion of pistons in their cylinders would create friction which could quickly burn them up if a lubricant were not provided. Similarly, the inward-outward motion of the male penis in the female vagina could cause discomfort and pain if adequate lubrication were missing. It is the function of Cowper's gland and of two glands in the woman's body to furnish such lubrication. The large intestine and anus serve no direct sexual function; they are shown in the diagram just to indicate their relationship to the sex organs.

How Sex Functions in Women

No less ingenious than the sexual equipment of men is that of women. It is shown in the next diagram. Mention has already been made of the vagina, the tube or passage through which sperm enter a woman's body; and, if she becomes pregnant, a fully developed child emerges from her body at the end of nine months. Similar to the male penis, the female vagina varies in size—not only from woman to woman but in the same woman, depending on whether or not she is sexually excited. The vagina expands much more slowly than the penis; but like the penis, it does enlarge when aroused.

No other part of the body has the automatic elasticity of the female reproductive apparatus. Before sexual intercourse has occurred, for example, the opening of the vagina is only about three-fourths of an inch in width; after some months of intercourse it has stretched to approximately an inch and a quarter; during childbirth it expands to five or six inches, then slowly returns to its normal size.

In a virgin—that is, a woman who has never experienced sexual intercourse—the mouth of the vagina is normally covered by a membrane called the hymen. The thickness and toughness of the hymen vary greatly. In many girls it becomes so stretched, even before intercourse, as to offer no resistance at all. If the hymen has not been broken or stretched in advance, it may cause slight pain and some bleeding the first time intercourse is experienced; this is nothing to fear. Only in rare instances is the hymen so leathery as to provide a major obstacle to intercourse, and even then medical help can alleviate any serious difficulty.

Ancient peoples believed that if the hymen was broken or stretched before her wedding night, this was certain evidence that the bride was not a virgin. In some cultures a white sheet was placed in the marriage bed, and unless it was stained with blood the following morning, the bride was assumed to have had intercourse before and was punished accordingly. While no one in our civilization is quite that crude, there are still some men who expect to find an unbroken hymen in their brides. They need to be reminded that the hymen can be stretched in several ways; the fact that it is broken does not constitute proof that a girl is not a virgin.

Near the outer lips of the vagina is a curious female organ called the clitoris. This is apparently a woman's vestigial remnant of the male penis. Exactly why she should have this remnant we do not know. Perhaps it is a reminder of the interesting fact that in some

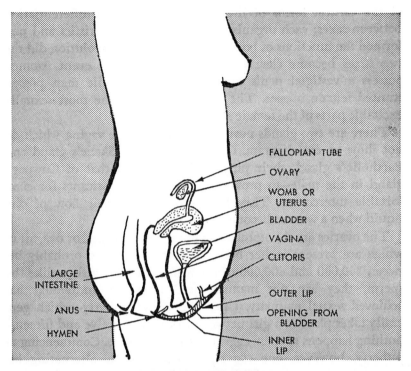

FALLOPIAN TUBE
OVARY
WOMB OR
UTERUS
BLADDER
VAGINA
CLITORIS

LARGE
INTESTINE

OUTER LIP

OPENING FROM
BLADDER

ANUS

HYMEN

INNER
LIP

THE FEMALE SEX ORGANS

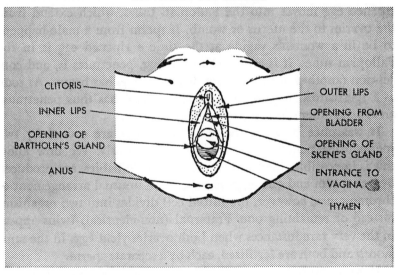

CLITORIS

INNER LIPS

OPENING OF
BARTHOLIN'S GLAND

ANUS

OUTER LIPS

OPENING FROM
BLADDER

OPENING OF
SKENE'S GLAND

ENTRANCE TO
VAGINA

HYMEN

Sex Is Here To Stay 111

of the earliest forms of life there was no sharp differentiation between sexes; each organism carried the characteristics and performed the functions of both sexes. Only later in evolution did the two sexes become clearly differentiated. In any event, women possess a vestigial penis called the clitoris, while men possess stunted female breasts. The clitoris is one of the most sexually excitable parts of the female anatomy.

There are two glands near the opening of the vagina which do not show on our diagram. Called respectively Skene's gland and Bartholin's gland, their purpose is similar to that of Cowper's gland in the male—to provide the necessary lubricants for comfortable intercourse. They begin to furnish their flow of oily liquid when a woman becomes sexually excited.

The ovaries are the storehouses for a woman's eggs, or ova, all of which are present in her body at birth. There are probably between 300,000 and 400,000 of them in each baby girl; unlike the sperm, they are not manufactured after the individual has achieved sexual maturity. Until the age of puberty—which generally takes place in a girl between the ages of twelve and fifteen—nothing happens to these eggs; they are just there. Commencing at puberty, however, one egg ripens each month—alternating between the two ovaries. This process is known as ovulation. The ripened egg moves into the Fallopian tubes, which extend from the ovaries to the uterus or womb. If sperm from a male happens to be in a woman's vagina at the time a ripened egg is in the Fallopian tubes, it is attracted to the egg, penetrates it, and conception (another term for onset of pregnancy) has begun. As soon as a spermatozoon (singular of spermatozoa) has thus penetrated an egg, no other spermatozoon is able to do so.

It was once believed that identical twins are caused by two spermatozoa penetrating an egg simultaneously. We now know this is impossible. Identical twins, like single babies, are produced by one sperm and one egg; because of an unusual arrangement of chromosomes, however, the initial cell divides into two organisms instead of remaining one. Fraternal (non-identical) twins appear in the very rare instances when both ovaries yield eggs in the same month and both are fertilized, each by a separate sperm.

If no sperm is present to fertilize the egg, it passes on down the vagina and is expelled from the body. No one has ever actually seen the egg as it leaves the body. It is less than one-hundredth of an inch in diameter; about three million of them could be accommodated in a thimble.

Unlike the male urethra, there is no one passage in a woman which carries both her urine and her sex secretions. It is only near the mouth of the vagina that the outlet from the bladder reaches the same general outer opening from her body.

Life Begins

When an egg has been fertilized, it then normally moves into the womb, which is to be its home for the ensuing nine months. Here it slowly develops into a human infant, obtaining all its nourishment from the body of the mother. It was once believed that the fertilized egg—or for that matter, even the spermatozoon before it reaches the egg—looked exactly like a miniature person, which only had to grow in size during the period of pregnancy. We now know this is not so. The cell which results from a sperm fertilizing an egg contains microscopic chromosomes and genes; it is these which carry the various characteristics and traits which the infant inherits from both his parents. As it slowly grows from one cell to a full human being, the foetus, as it is called, retraces some of the steps which life generally followed in its development through evolution. At one early stage, it resembles a fish. Later it assumes the appearance of an amphibian, then an ape, and finally, a human being.

The womb is the best possible hostess for the developing life it harbors. It is so anxious to perform its duties well that each month it prepares for a possible guest. As ovulation is about to take place, the walls of the womb thicken with extra blood supply, ready to feed the fertilized egg if it arrives. If no such guest makes an appearance that month, the nourishment provided in advance becomes unnecessary, sloughs off the walls of the womb and passes out through the vagina. This process is called menstruation. A woman menstruates each month unless she is pregnant. A small quantity of blood—usually half a cup or less—along with some of the mucus from the uterus wall, flows out of her body.

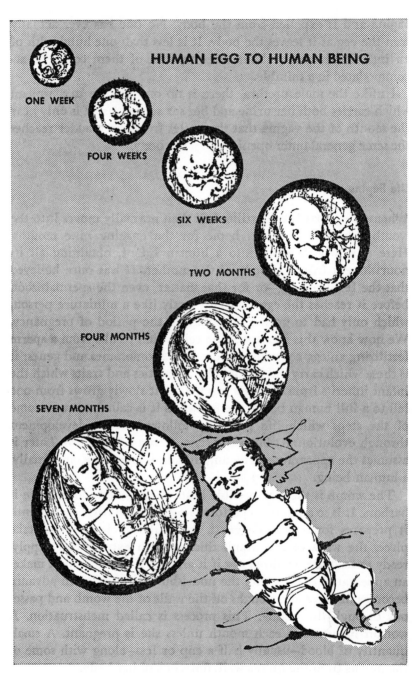

HUMAN EGG TO HUMAN BEING

ONE WEEK

FOUR WEEKS

SIX WEEKS

TWO MONTHS

FOUR MONTHS

SEVEN MONTHS

Here is another of the marvelous provisions of nature to which we have already referred. You know that blood always tends to clot as it flows from the human body. Were this not so, we would risk bleeding to death from every nosebleed or scratch. If, on the other hand, menstrual blood were to clot, it would block the vaginal passage, make the bearing of children impossible, ultimately causing infection and death. The only normal circumstance we know of in which blood flowing from an opening in the human body does not clot is in the process of menstruation!

Menstruation can last anywhere from a couple of days to about a week. While it is occurring a girl can pretty much go about her normal routine of activity except that she wears a protective napkin or tampon.

Some girls find the days preceding and during menstruation to be difficult emotionally. They may be unusually tense or easily aroused to anger or tears at this time. A considerate fiancé or husband will try to be especially tender and considerate where this is the case. Many girls prefer to avoid such strenuous exercise as swimming while they are menstruating. If a girl who usually enjoys activity of this kind seems on occasion mysteriously unwilling to participate, a wise boy gets the point without asking embarrassing questions.

It was once universally believed that there is something unlucky or unclean about a menstruating woman. It was therefore considered dangerous to have any contact with her. This may be, in part, the origin of separating the sexes in an Orthodox synagogue. After all, one could never tell which women might be menstruating at a given religious service. Even so enlightened and intelligent a rabbi as Nachmanides wrote, in the thirteenth century:

> It appears to me that in days of yore menstruating women were totally sundered from society. They were not allowed to come near anyone, or to speak to anyone, for the ancients knew that their very breath is harmful. It seems that they were kept separate in a tent which was out of bounds to everyone else. Here is a saying in the talmudic tractate נדה Niddah (the Hebrew term meaning a menstruating woman): "One may not touch a

נדה ." R. Yohanan says: "It is forbidden to walk behind her, or to tread on the ground where she has trodden. It is likewise forbidden to make use of her labor."

Today we recognize all this to be sheer superstition. Ancient peoples are not to be condemned; they were operating with the limited knowledge of their time. There is no excuse, however, for a modern person to believe such nonsense. A menstruating woman, provided she follows simple rules of hygiene to keep herself clean, is living through a perfectly natural phase of her life. She should be treated (and should treat herself) as normally as possible, and is no more to be shunned or avoided than a person with a nosebleed.

Just as some boys begin to produce sperm earlier or later than the average, so there are girls whose menstruation commences sooner or later than in most cases. Usually a woman continues to menstruate monthly until she reaches the age of about forty-five to fifty-five. The stage at which menstruation gradually ceases is called menopause or change of life. Thereafter, it is impossible for a woman to become pregnant. She can continue, however, to enjoy an active sex life with her husband.

The Greatest Wonder of All

Nothing on earth is more beautiful or important than the fact that a man and woman who truly, deeply love each other can, through the expression and consummation of that love, create a new human being. Nature has provided for the survival of all its species of life through reproduction. But nowhere is this process as meaningful as in human life.

It is, of course, through sexual intercourse—also called coitus— that humans become parents. The enlarged and stiffened penis is inserted into the vagina which is also made large enough, through stimulation, to receive it. It is then moved back and forth, with increasing excitement, until the male comes to a climax known as an orgasm. When this happens there is an ejaculation of semen in spurts. The contact between penis and vagina causes an orgasm in the woman too, with much the same pleasurable physical sensation, but with no ejaculation.

Each spermatozoon is so small that ten thousand or more, placed side by side, would cover less than an inch. Each also has a lashing tail which propels it up into the vagina in the direction of the Fallopian tubes. If there is a ripened egg waiting there and just one spermatozoon penetrates it, pregnancy has begun. If not, the sperm gradually dry up or drain out of the vagina.

Primitive peoples of course practiced sexual intercourse and the women became pregnant, but they failed to establish a connection between the two. They invented a number of fanciful explanations to account for pregnancies. A tribe in Eastern Australia still believes that girl babies are fashioned by the moon, boy babies by the wood lizard. In Queensland it is commonly supposed that the thunder-god makes babies from swamp mud and puts them into a woman's womb. Elsewhere it is believed that a woman becomes pregnant through sitting over a fire on which a certain kind of fish has been roasted, or because she has successfully hunted for a particular species of frog.

In animal life below the human level conception takes place in one of several ways. In some, especially certain fish, the female lays eggs outside her body, the male comes along shortly afterward and, without even seeing the female, deposits over the eggs a substance from his own body without which they cannot become fertilized. In other animals, the male injects a fluid from his body into that of the female while the egg is still forming within her body and before the shell has appeared. The fertilizing element thus becomes a part of the egg itself, so that after it is laid, only the attention of the female is needed in order for the egg to hatch. In a number of species the male is almost incidental; once he injects the necessary fluid for fertilization into the female, either she devours him (literally!) or he goes off to die by himself.

Intercourse among human beings differs in a number of very important ways from the same phenomenon in other animals. Among these differences are the following:

1. Only among humans do the male and female generally face and see each other during the act of intercourse.

2. Only among humans does intercourse serve purposes other

than propagation of the race. It is doubtful whether females other than women are even capable of experiencing an orgasm. Intercourse in the rest of the animal kingdom occurs only when the female is ready to be impregnated and only for the purpose of pregnancy. Intercourse in human life occurs when a husband and wife who love each other want thus to express their love. And in addition to the fact that it sometimes results in pregnancy, at all times in a good marriage it increases the very love which it expresses.

3. Only among humans does intercourse have a spiritual as well as a physical aspect. Only with us does it lead to the formation of families and the creation of a kind of love which endures even beyond the time of life when intercourse between husband and wife is possible.

4. Thus far we have mentioned only those respects in which sex is a more wonderful and exalted experience among humans than in any other branch of life. There is one respect, however, in which it can also be more degrading. We are the only species in which the male can sometimes overpower the female, forcing her to have intercourse against her will. Forced coitus is called rape. What it means, plainly and simply, is that sex in human life can be either immeasurably glorious or unforgivably depraved. The choice is ours.

Additional Problems

Only human beings are capable, if they wish, of preventing intercourse from resulting in pregnancy. This is referred to as birth control or contraception. It can be accomplished in several ways. The most common are:

(a) for the male to wear a thin sheath called a condom on his penis to prevent any sperm from entering the vagina;

(b) for the female to insert a diaphragm which covers the opening between the vagina and the uterus, thus preventing sperm from fertilizing a ripened egg;

(c) to insert a medicinal jelly into the vagina which can kill sperm without injuring her;

(d) to use a contraceptive foam which, if injected into the vagina before intercourse, can kill sperm;

(e) to have a physician insert a small metal or plastic ring in the womb which, for some reason we do not yet fully understand, seems to make conception impossible; or

(f) for the female to take a pill which prevents ovulation, thus making it impossible for an egg to be fertilized. The pill, however, is taken not just in anticipation of each act of intercourse, but for twenty days of each month under the direction of a physician; otherwise it is not dependable. Actually, there is no one known method of birth control which is always sure.

One of the least reliable methods is the so-called rhythm system. This system is based on the fact that there are certain days in the menstrual cycle when there is no ripened egg present, hence no possibility of becoming pregnant. While this is true, there is enough variation in ovulation and menstruation in any one woman to make the calculation of this safe period so complicated that it cannot be used with any great assurance.

Another extremely unreliable method which some couples foolishly use is called withdrawal. This means commencing coitus but not completing it; as soon as the male feels his orgasm beginning, he quickly withdraws his penis from the vagina to prevent sperm from entering the woman's body. In addition to the fact that this is an unhealthfully frustrating practice for both sexes, it is unreliable as a method of birth control because sometimes semen begins to flow from the penis even before the actual orgasm. The attraction of sperm for a ripened egg, moreover, is so great that even when deposited outside a woman's body, near the lips of her vagina, they can swim toward the Fallopian tubes and cause conception. There have been women who became pregnant in this manner without actually experiencing intercourse.

Can a pregnancy be terminated before birth after the egg has been fertilized? Yes, by a surgical procedure known as abortion. There are certain conditions which necessitate abortion in order to save the mother's life. If performed at the proper stage of pregnancy, by a reputable physician in a good hospital, abortions can be successful. But the performance of abortions without medical reasons—just to terminate a pregnancy—is illegal in every state of our nation. No doctor can perform this operation without risking imprisonment. As a consequence, when they are done, it is usually by medically incompetent persons under poor hygienic circumstances. The danger under these conditions is extremely high; a large percentage of attempts leads to serious infection, inability ever to have children and even death.

Aside from the medical danger involved in abortion, there is a serious moral question too. Although, as we shall see in our next chapter, Judaism and some other faiths differ in their attitude toward birth control, they are in agreement that abortion—except where necessary on advice of a physician, to save a woman's life—is reprehensible. Many Jews would also justify abortion to avert the birth of a defective child. Most Catholics would not. We Jews believe in general that there is a vast difference morally between preventing conception and terminating a life which has already commenced. Some people feel so strongly on this matter that they would classify abortion as murder.

> If an infant were deliberately killed one day after birth, would this be murder? What if it were killed a week before birth? What bearing do these questions have on abortion? Do you believe abortion is justifiable where there is reason to suspect the child may be abnormal? Why?

Worry over masturbation has caused perhaps as much needless anguish as any other phase of sex life among human beings. Masturbation refers to the fondling of the penis by a male or of the clitoris by a female to the point of having an orgasm without coitus. Medical authorities are agreed that no harm results from this practice. A generation or more ago, parents frequently frightened their children with threats that masturbation could cause physical or mental illness, that it was a sin, or that it could make them incapable of enjoying a normal sex life and having children in later years. None of this is true. The greatest possible harm from masturbation springs from feelings of guilt about it, and such feelings are unwarranted. It has been estimated that over ninety per cent of all boys and perhaps as many as sixty per cent of the girls masturbate at some point in their lives; some men and women do even after they are married, at times when their wives or husbands are unavailable. Since masturbation is self-stimulation, it cannot possibly express or deepen one's love for his mate, as intercourse does. But neither is it harmful.

There is no mention of masturbation in the Bible. It was, to be sure, condemned by later Jewish authorities—as it was by the leaders of most religions—but clearly on the basis of insufficient knowledge of the facts.

An abnormal sexual problem which requires brief comment in this chapter is homosexuality. This refers to a small percentage of adults who derive their sexual stimulation and pleasure from partners of the same rather than the opposite sex. There are also those who derive sexual excitement from contacts with both sexes. We already know that all of us grow through a period early in our lives when we are attracted primarily to others of our own sex. We have seen too that all males have some female characteristics (breasts, for example), while all females have certain male traits (the clitoris, for example). The best medical opinion today is that the homosexual suffers from arrested physical and mental growth, that he has never emerged from an earlier stage of development to the point of a mature sex life, that there are more female traits in the male or more male traits in the female than there should be. Homosexuality is a sickness. Those who suffer from it should be understood and, if possible, cured, not condemned or scorned. A young person who has reason to suspect a tendency toward homosexuality in himself should seek the help of someone whom he can fully trust—a parent, his rabbi, doctor, a teacher, or psychiatrist. The earlier in life such a condition is discovered and treatment begun, the better is the prognosis for cure.

Path of Wisdom

There is almost no sexual problem that cannot be solved if faced honestly and with competent help. There are many which can become bothersome if allowed to fester without adequate help. For this reason we would encourage you to discuss whatever problems of this kind you may have with an older person. It does little good to talk about them only to others your own age. Those who talk loudest and boldest are seldom the ones who really know the most.

The wise thing for each young couple to do as their marriage date approaches is to schedule one or more pre-marital conferences—one with their rabbi, another with a physician, preferably a gynecologist, a doctor who specializes in the female reproductive and sexual system. The rabbi will discuss the spiritual aspects of marriage. The physician will examine both bride and groom, discuss with them any problems of sexual adjustment he thinks they may encounter, give them the birth control information they need, and try honestly and helpfully to answer their questions.

For Instance

A. The Education Committee of the temple was meeting to discuss a course in Preparation for Marriage which the rabbi proposed to give to juniors and seniors of the High School Department. This book was to be the text; each member of the Committee had been provided with a copy in advance, and they all had read it.

While most members of the Committee were enthusiastically in favor of the course and thanked the rabbi for his suggestion that it be given, some had serious misgivings. One said, for example: "I'm not a prude, but I must admit that certain pages of this book embarrassed me; I wouldn't want my seventeen-year-old daughter to read them. It's all right to give our high school youngsters sex information in general, but I don't approve of going into such minute detail. The diagrams especially bothered me. Can't we leave anything to the imagination?"

"I agree," another member said eagerly. "What bothers me even more is the information given in Chapter Eight about birth control. Don't you think it's time enough for young people to learn about such things when they are ready for marriage? I don't mind telling you I'm even worried a little that this kind of information may encourage some of our boys and girls to go farther sexually than they otherwise would."

This last comment evoked vigorous disagreement from one woman on the committee. "Oh no," she exclaimed, "how can you even think such a thing? Our boys and girls come from decent, ethical homes, where they have been taught the difference between right and wrong. I can't believe that any of them would violate the sex ethics they have been taught by their parents. As a matter of fact, my objection to this course is that sex education belongs in the home, not in the religious school. We shouldn't usurp the rights of parents."

"I don't agree with any of these objections," said the newest member of the committee. "I like the idea of the course and I approve the book. My only suggestion would be that certain chapters or parts of them should be taught separately to boys and girls. I think, for example, that if the diagrams and discussions on the male and female sex organs were covered in separate groups—with the rabbi teaching the boys and a woman physician or nurse instructing the girls—there would be less embarrassment. Otherwise, I'm all for it!"

> What would your reactions be if you were on this committee? Would you have voted for or against the course? Why? How would you have responded to each of the arguments summarized above? Are there other objections which could have been voiced at this meeting? How could they be answered?

B. After Professor Magoun had finished a lecture to a group of Jewish high school students which included much of the information of this chapter, he invited written questions, which he then proceeded to answer. These, of course, were anonymous. One student wrote the following: "I find that your method of analyzing and describing the sexual process in front of a large group goes against my moral sense. It seems immoral and disgusting to speak of these matters in such a way. Perhaps between two or three people it would be more natural, but this does not seem correct."

> How do you feel about this reaction? Do you agree or disagree? Do you think this student would have felt better if he (or she) had first read this book, then come together in

a large group to discuss it? What would you be inclined to guess about the questioner's knowledge of sex? About his (or her) sexual conduct and future sex adjustment?

C. Chet and Jane had been engaged for ten months, had set the date of their wedding, and had already seen the rabbi for a premarital conference. At his suggestion, they had also gone to see a gynecologist who had talked to both of them and examined Jane. Up to that time everything had gone very well; since that day, however, the roof had caved in.

While the gynecologist was discussing birth control with them, he said it would be possible for him to fit Jane for a diaphragm and give it to her to take with them on their honeymoon. Chet flushed perceptibly, though neither Jane nor the doctor noticed it. On the way home he was silent and sullen. Jane's efforts to find out what was wrong proved fruitless. Later that night when they were alone, Chet finally told her what had been bothering him. He knew, he said, that a girl whose hymen is unbroken cannot be fitted for a diaphragm. Several of his friends who were already married had told him that their brides had been advised by their physicians to return after the honeymoon to obtain a diaphragm, but that in the meantime some other method of birth control would have to be used temporarily.

To Chet this could mean only one thing: Jane was not a virgin. If her hymen was broken or stretched and her vagina was large enough for a diaphragm to be fitted, he was convinced that she must already have experienced intercourse with someone else. Whenever they had talked together about sex, both had said they had never had intercourse, nor did they want to with each other until after the wedding. Chet still loved Jane very much, but he did not see how he could marry her or they could be happy after she had deceived him in one of the most important areas of life.

> How would you have felt had you been in Chet's place? What would you have said or done in Jane's place? Who was at fault? Could this situation have been avoided? Would any argument now convince Chet? Would you advise them to go ahead with their wedding plans or to call the whole thing off?

D. Gail, who is thirteen years old, has not yet commenced to menstruate. She has been told all about it by her mother and older sister but is extremely apprehensive about the fact that some time in the fairly near future she will no doubt have her own first experience. As long as she can remember, her mother and sister have called their periods "the curse." For days before each flow starts and until it is just about finished, they have complained about being depressed and feeling a variety of aches and pains. Gail's mother usually spends three or four days in bed each month at that time.

Gail has heard many arguments between her parents and remembers occasions on which her mother complained to her father bitterly about "the curse," saying that no man could ever appreciate what a woman has to endure just because she is a woman.

As a consequence of all this, Gail isn't happy about being a girl and having to face the prospect of menstruating for many years. She looks with envy at her brother Bob, knowing that he will never have this worry.

> How wholesome or realistic is Gail's attitude? Who is to blame for it? Are her mother and sister justified in resenting the inconvenience and discomfort of menstruation? Is there anything that could be done to help Gail? Why do some women find their periods so much more difficult than others?

E. Meanwhile, unknown to Gail, Bob has his own problems. It was just about a year ago that he had his first "wet dream." He awakened in the middle of the night—only half aware at first of the fact that he had just been interrupted in the midst of an exciting dream about sex. As soon as he became almost fully awakened, he realized that some kind of liquid had emerged from his penis. At first he thought perhaps his bladder control had failed, but this didn't seem probable at his age and anyway it soon became apparent that the liquid was not urine. That was the only time Bob has awakened during such a dream, but on several occasions since then he has found stains in the morning on his pajamas and sheets. This embarrasses him; he wonders whether his mother and the maid have noticed them.

The first time this happened, Bob began to worry that there was something wrong with him, that the liquid which came from his penis during the night was the semen he had heard about; but the fact that it was leaking out must mean that he would never be able to live a normal sex life or have children. This had become almost an obsession, usurping his mind even at times when he tried to study or read. The one boy friend with whom he had tried to talk about it told him this just meant that he needed sexual intercourse and should try to find a girl who would be willing to try it with him. Then his semen wouldn't have to escape as it had during the night. But Bob was afraid to follow this advice; he continued to have occasional nocturnal emissions and continued to worry. At times he wished he were a girl so that, like Gail, he wouldn't have to face such a problem.

> Could Bob's worries have been prevented? Was his friend's advice sound? If you were Bob, what would you do? If you gave him this chapter to read, would that resolve the situation? What can you tell about their parents and home life from the feelings of Bob and Gail?

Chapter NINE

DO ALL RELIGIONS AGREE ON SEX?

THE ONLY HONEST ANSWER TO THE QUESTION WHICH HEADS THIS chapter is *no*. There are many aspects of sex, to be sure, on which all the religions with which we are familiar in the United States are in substantial agreement. There are others, however, on which there is considerable disagreement. In discussing both the similarities and the differences, we shall be concerned only with those religions which are usually found among our neighbors and friends, which means to say: Judaism, Catholicism and the various Protestant faiths.

It would be foolish to pretend that there is one Jewish attitude toward sex or one Christian point of view. While Catholics come closer to unanimity than any other group, even among them there are some differences of opinion on sex. Still—as we examine the

127

historical record—it is possible to discern major divergences between what may be called the main Jewish and the main Christian points of view.

Christianity on Sex

Generally speaking, Christianity through much of its history has been negative and suspicious in its approach to sex. Unlike nearly all the biblical and talmudic leaders of Judaism, so far as we know, Jesus was never married. In order to divorce him from any possible taint of connection with sex, Christian tradition even resorted to the belief that Jesus was born to a virgin. Paul, who was the real founder of Christianity, looked upon sexual desire and especially coitus as evil. He expressed the wish that all men might be capable, as he was, of remaining celibate (male virgins). Because he realized that most were not, as a concession to human weakness he said: "It is better to marry than to burn."[1] Scholars are not sure whether he meant better than to "burn with sexual desires" or to "burn in hell" for indulging in intercourse without marriage. What is certain, however, is that he looked upon sexual relations with disdain.

His attitude carried over into most of the early history of Christianity. Summarizing his view and that of the New Testament generally, one Christian authority has written: "In this idea of marriage as an accommodation to human weakness and a hindrance to the fullest service of God there is but little appreciation of its dignity and high calling; nor do the writers of the New Testament show much sense of the joys and privileges of family life . . ."[2] The same writer, in commenting on the preponderant Christian attitude in the centuries following the completion of the New Testament, has said: "While none denied that marriage, relatively speaking, was a good thing, it was nevertheless tolerated rather than commended." Also: "Of the joys, privileges and opportunities of home and family life we find little appreciation, while hardly more than lip-service is paid to the blessing of children."[3]

On rare occasions a voice of protest or disagreement was raised within the church; but generally, a negative view of sex and a rather reluctant acceptance of intercourse within marriage as a concession to human weakness and the only means of propagating the race prevailed. These were the characteristic outlooks of Christianity throughout most of its history. One evidence of this is that in some Christian denominations—most notably but not exclusively Roman Catholicism—religious leadership is limited to men and women who do not indulge in what we would consider to be a normal sex life. Thus do these faiths indicate their conviction that the highest form of human life is that of the celibate and the virgin.

In the extreme Christian view, sex desire and its fulfillment within marriage were considered scarcely more ethical. St. Jerome, for example, wrote: "He who loves his own wife too ardently is an adulterer." St. Augustine said: "Intercourse even with one's legitimate wife is unlawful and wicked where the conception of offspring is prevented." In a similar vein, the church fathers condemned the use of cosmetics and other adornments by all women, on the ground that these might increase their sexual attractiveness in the eyes of men. According to Tertullian, even the natural, unadorned beauty of women "ought to be obliterated by concealment and neglect, since it is dangerous to those who look upon it."[4]

Saint Augustine even attempted to read his own views of sex back into the minds and lives of the Hebrew Patriarchs, Abraham, Isaac and Jacob. He said they would have preferred to fulfill God's commandment to "be fruitful and multiply" without indulging in coitus, but this was manifestly impossible. He assumed, therefore, that they experienced intercourse with their wives only reluctantly, and as a duty.

There is no evidence in the world to indicate that Augustine was correct about the feelings he attributed to the Patriarchs. The Christian views on sex cited above would have been impossible within Judaism. They have been gradually abandoned in modern times by many Christian groups too. It is now increasingly accepted by the leaders of a large number of Christian denominations that an active sex life between husbands and wives is a good thing, even apart from their desire to have children. Insofar as they have come to this point of view, however, it is important to recognize that they have moved away from the historic position of Christianity on sex and toward that of Judaism.

Judaism on Sex

What has the Jewish view been? For the most part, that sexual intercourse between husbands and wives is a good thing—desirable and wholesome—intended by God not only as a means of creating succeeding generations, but also to fortify and reinforce the love of married couples. True, there is an occasional expression within authentic Judaism which sounds suspiciously like Christianity, but this is the exception rather than the rule. The following statement by Maimonides is a particularly curious and rare one: "We ought to limit sexual intercourse altogether, hold it in contempt, and desire it only rarely . . . The act is too base to be performed except when needed."[5]

Much closer to Jewish tradition is the rebuttal to this statement uttered in the next century by another authoritative spokesman for Judaism, Nachmanides: "It is not true, as our rabbi and master asserted in his *Guide for the Perplexed,* praising Aristotle for teaching that the sexual urge is a source of shame to us. God forbid that the truth should be in accordance with the teachings of the Greek! . . . The act of sexual union is holy and pure . . . The Lord created all things in accordance with His wisdom, and whatever He created cannot possibly be shameful or ugly . . . When a man is in union with his wife in a spirit of holiness and purity, the Divine Presence is with them."[6]

> How can we determine who was closer to the view of authentic Judaism on sex—Maimonides or Nachmanides? Does it make any difference?

One of the shorter books of the Bible is devoted in its entirety to the physical side of love. True, in Jewish tradition *The Song of Songs* was looked upon as an allegory depicting the love of God and the Jewish people for each other. But there can be no doubt that it was originally written as a series of passionate love songs. It contains the very beautiful words you may have heard in an Israeli song or seen engraved on wedding rings: דוֹדִי לִי וַאֲנִי לוֹ (*dodi li va-ani lo;* my beloved is mine and I am his). In this book are also to be found descriptions of a woman in pursuit of her loved one (3:1–4), of her physical beauty as seen by him (4:1–5), and of his beauty as it impresses her (5:8–16).

Both Bible and Talmud describe and discuss matters of sex with uninhibited honesty. King David is portrayed as having indulged in intercourse with the wife of another man and being punished for it. In the Talmud there is an interesting discussion as to the best time for a man and his wife to have intercourse. Our tradition even includes a suggested prayer of considerable meaning and beauty, to be recited by a man before coitus with his wife. Rabbinic literature recognizes the fact that the sex urge varies from person to person, that consequently one man may require intercourse more frequently than another. According to the *Shulchan Aruch,* "each man is obliged to perform his marital duty according to his strength and according to his occupation. Gentlemen of leisure should perform their marital obligation every night. Laborers who are employed in the city where they reside should perform their duty twice weekly, but if they are employed in another city, once a week. Donkey-drivers [should have marital relations] once a week; camel-drivers, once in thirty days; sailors, once in six months. As for scholars, it is obligatory for them to have intercourse once a week, and it is customary for this to be on Friday nights."[7]

> How can we account for this passage? On what basis did Jewish authorities decide how often men in different occupations should have intercourse with their wives? Is there any validity to their reasoning?

Unlike many ancient and medieval cultures, in which only men were deemed to have sexual desires, Judaism recognized the sexual needs of women and insisted that they be satisfied. Thus a husband was forbidden to leave on a long journey without first having intercourse with his wife, and was enjoined to have intercourse with her again as soon as possible after his return. The bridegroom

Do All Religions Agree on Sex? 131

was bidden to be respectful of his wife's natural timidity in their first performance of coitus: "The Torah teaches gentle manners: the bridegroom should not enter the marriage chamber until the bride gives him leave."[8] Contrary to the strictures of Christianity against the use of cosmetics by women, Meir of Rothenburg, the outstanding rabbi of the thirteenth century, said: "Let a curse descend upon a woman who has a husband and does not strive to be attractive."[9]

Intercourse between husband and wife, according to Judaism, must always be a beautiful experience. Every form of sex-play between them which helped to make it so was approved. The same Maimonides whose curious, almost un-Jewish statement on sex has already been quoted, said elsewhere: "The sexual union should be consummated only out of desire and as the result of the joy of the husband and wife . . . He must not approach her when he thinks of another woman and certainly not when he is under the influence of alcohol or while they are quarreling and hatred divides them. He must not approach her against her will or force her to submit to him out of fear."[10] In the final portion of this statement Maimonides was simply reiterating a view which the Talmud had expressed many centuries earlier: "He who coerces his wife will produce unworthy children."[11]

Another rabbi of talmudic times urged that each act of coitus between husband and wife be as exciting and fresh as was the first on their wedding night.[12] Finally, Judaism demonstrated long ago a truth which many among us are learning only now: that active sex interest and sex life between married mates is to continue beyond the wife's ability to bear children. Even if a man and woman young enough to have children know that it will never be possible for them to have children together, it is still legitimate for them to marry and enjoy intercourse.

The teachings of some religions in regard to sex make it very difficult for young people in those denominations to cope with their own feelings of sexual desire. Adolescence, after all, is a time of increasing sexual interest. It marks the emergence of a person from childhood into adulthood—the time when all the organs and glands of the body are ripening for full use in marriage. At such a time it would be unnatural for any of us not to feel a strong physical attraction for the opposite sex. To tell a young person that it is wrong to feel what nature itself impels him to feel is to create an almost intolerable problem for him.

Judaism helps us face this difficult but wonderful period of life in a wholesome way. It tells us we should not feel guilty over our strong feelings of sexual desire; if God did not want us to experience such sensations, he would have created us differently. Judaism teaches that life is good and sex is good—if we accept it and learn how to control and use it for our advantage and richest growth.

Clearly, then, there has been major disagreement between Judaism and Christianity regarding sex. The fact that today the difference is less than it once was is a tribute to the ancient insight of our tradition, almost from the time of its inception. It would be dishonest to pretend that every Jew in the world knows or follows the traditional attitude of our faith toward sex. Those who do, however, can live a healthier and more wholesome life, with greater probability of happiness in their marriages.

Debate on Birth Control

One consequence of these differences on sex in general has been a wide disagreement on birth control. The natural result of the old Christian belief that sex is a necessary evil and coitus is permissible only as a means to conceive children was a strong opposition to any method of contraception which would enable married couples to enjoy intercourse for its own sake, without intending to produce a child. Originally, both Catholics and Protestants were opposed to birth control. Among Protestants there has been a steady inclination toward change, so that many of the leading Protestant denominations, as they have moved closer to our Jewish view of sex in general, have also relaxed their antagonism to birth control.

The change in the Roman Catholic Church has been slower and less substantial. At first the church taught that under no circumstances did a married couple have the right to cohabit (another term for coitus) without intending pregnancy as a consequence.

More recently, however, Catholic authorities have moved to the point where they approve the so-called rhythm method, which we described in our last chapter. This they accept as being a *natural* method of family planning. All other methods they consider *artificial* and to be condemned. There have been suggestions, some even from within the Catholic Church, that perhaps the contraceptive pill may in time be approved as *natural*. As this is being written, the matter is still under church study; there has been no change thus far in official Catholic opposition to the pill and all other techniques of birth control which are deemed to be *artificial*.

In the modern Jewish view this distinction between two kinds of contraception is not valid. Even the Talmud recognized certain circumstances under which the practice of birth control was recommended. The methods then known were nowhere near as sophisticated or certain as ours, but the principle was identical. Judaism believed then—and does now—that the noblest fulfillment of a marriage is the birth and rearing of children. It believes equally, however, that God created us with sexual desires and needs because He considered these to be good; and that partners in marriage should live as full a sex life as they desire, utilizing whatever methods they wish for birth control in order that they can continue to express their love in intercourse without producing more children than they want or can properly love.

Are Sex and Love the Same?

If Judaism was wise in anticipating many of the insights of modern psychology in terms of sex generally, it was no less perceptive with regard to the relationship between sex and love. We have already referred to the truth that a good sexual adjustment is more the consequence of love than its cause. Some people have from time to time considered sex to be just a psychological tension—similar to an itch which is to be scratched in the most convenient way, or to hunger which is to be satisfied by whatever edible food happens to be available. Such an attitude, in addition to being inaccurate, is unworthy of human beings as physical-spiritual creatures. On the simplest level, it overlooks the fact that men have developed polite manners to govern even certain forms of scratching and eating.

It also ignores the fundamental truth that human sexual intercourse is a delicately balanced combination of physical-plus-emotional-plus-mental-plus-spiritual factors, none of which can be emphasized without regard for the other. It simply is not true, as was once believed, that a good sexual adjustment between husband and wife will always lead to a good marriage. While no one can deny that—given two normal, healthy young people—a good marriage is not very likely without a mutually satisfying sexual adjustment, much more than that is needed. Dr. Erich Fromm, the world renowned psychoanalyst, has understood and expressed this as well as anyone: "Love is not the result of sexual satisfaction, but sexual happiness . . . is the result of love."[13]

Sexual satisfaction can be good or bad, desirable or degrading, wholesome or diseased. Intercourse can be an expression of love or of something quite the opposite of love. Another prominent psychiatrist, Dr. Karl Menninger, has stated this truth with dramatic effectiveness:

> The orgasm of a terrified soldier in battle, that of a loving husband in the arms of his wife, that of a desperate homosexual trying to improve his masculinity, and that of a violent and sadistic brute raping a child are not the same phenomena. The muscles and nerves and secretions may be the same but the orgasms are not the same, and the sexuality is not the same.[14]

He might have added, as we have already had occasion to observe, that the choice among these various kinds and degrees of sexuality is up to each individual. Only the proper choice can lead to a happy, successful marriage.

Judaism has excelled in understanding the subtle but intensely important relationship between sex and love in a good marriage. It must be more than a verbal accident that the Bible uses the word יָדַע yada—meaning knew—to describe intercourse. Thus we read, in Genesis: "And the man knew Eve his wife; and she conceived and bore Cain . . ." Intercourse on the human level was meant by God and nature to be something more than just physical contact and satisfaction. It involves two people *knowing* each other—respecting and caring for each other deeply in both physical and spiritual dimensions—loving each other enough to desire a permanent sharing of their lives, including partnership in the creation of new lives.

What Judaism knew to be true regarding man's love of God is also true of his love for the one woman in his life. "Thou shalt love the Lord thy God with all thy heart, with all thy soul and with all thy might." Only a whole person can love God. And only a whole person can truly love a husband or wife. In a play about an adolescent boy called *The Happy Time*, by Samuel Taylor, the boy's grandfather put it this way: "To be a man, one must learn to use the glands, the heart and the mind all together."

For Instance

A. Mark's parents are members of a fundamentalist Protestant sect which accepts every word of the Bible as being literally true. They believe that smoking, drinking and card playing are all serious sins. They are equally convinced that sex is evil and they disapprove of all physical expressions of affection between men and women.

Mark had grown up without questioning his parents' ideas. They had never really bothered him until he fell in love with Sally, whose thoughts about sex were very different from his. Sally's family is Protestant too but they belong to a liberal church. Their attitude toward sex is similar to that of Judaism as you have come to know it in this chapter.

Sally and Mark had discussed their differences regarding sex a number of times, especially since they became formally engaged last spring. Though they are no closer to agreement now than in the beginning, Sally isn't particularly worried. She is confident that, as she puts it, "nature will settle the argument," and that Mark will want to express his love for her sexually after they are married.

If you were a marriage counselor and this couple came to you, what advice would you give them? What do you think is their chance for a happy marriage? What makes people feel about sex the way Mark and his parents do? Is Sally correct in her confidence that things will take care of themselves after their wedding?

B. Mrs. Langfort—despite the fact that she has been married over twenty years and has given birth to two children—is convinced that sex is evil. She insists we can see this at the very beginning of the Bible, in the story of Adam and Eve. "At first they were naked in the Garden of Eden and didn't even realize that it made any difference—isn't that so?" she asks rather demandingly. "Then, after they had eaten of the tree of the knowledge of good and evil, and for the first time became aware of their nakedness, they were expelled from Eden, isn't that so? Well, what more proof do you need that God knew sex was evil when He first created it?"

Mrs. Langfort has taught her views of sex to her children and practically forced them on her husband. Because of her feelings she will not permit her sixteen-year-old daughter to be alone with a boy. She is afraid the girl may not be able to resist the temptation that may confront her. She permits her to date only if at least one other couple goes too, and she will not allow her to bring a date into the house at the end of the evening.

Are the facts of the Adam and Eve story correct as Mrs. Langfort recounts them? Is her interpretation of the facts accurate? How, if at all, would you answer her on this point? Is it possible for a Jewish woman to feel this way? What kind of marriage would you suppose Mr. and Mrs. Langfort have had? What kind of marriage would you predict for their daughter? How would you feel if you were their daughter? What would you do?

C. Phil and Madeline have been married five years. Their sex life has been good; they both enjoy intercourse and both experience orgasms practically every time. Yet they spend an increasing amount of time arguing and fighting. Sometimes it seems the only time they agree on anything is when they are in bed. In the past couple of years Madeline has been using sex as a weapon, warning

Phil that if he doesn't do as she asks, give her what she wants, she will deny him the sex he wants next time. He on his part becomes furious when she threatens him this way. "Don't act as if you were doing me the biggest favor in the world!" he practically shouts at her. "Sex is something to which I'm entitled, not a gift you can give or withhold as you please. Anyway, you're not the only woman in the world; if you don't want to satisfy my needs, I can find someone who will!"

> Does it sound realistic for a couple that quarrels so much to find mutual pleasure in their sex life? How good would you say their marriage is? In what ways is it good? In what ways not? Does a woman have the right to use sex for punishment and reward as Madeline has done? Do you blame Phil for reacting as he does? Why?

D. Kathy's parents had been opposed from the beginning to her match with Stan. Devout Catholics, they would by far have preferred their daughter to marry within her own church. After almost a year of opposition, however, they relented—especially since Kathy had successfully urged Stan to have a church wedding and to promise that their children would be educated as Catholics.

It seemed that the only remaining issue was the question of birth control. Kathy made it clear that, in accordance with the teachings of her church, she would accept no method of contraception except the rhythm method. She agreed with Stan that they could not afford to have children for several years at least, but said she would feel guilty discarding her religious principles in so important a matter. Stan said he supposed one method of birth control was about as good as another. If this was what Kathy wanted, it was all right with him. So they agreed that they would have sex relations after their marriage only at such times as Kathy was "safe" from becoming pregnant.

> With all important possible disputes apparently ironed out in advance, do you think Kathy and Stan could anticipate a good marriage? What issues can you see that might cause them trouble? Is Stan apt to be happy for the indefinite future with their solution to the problem of contraception? Why? Is the problem permanently solved for Kathy? Why?

Chapter TEN

WHY WAIT?

AN ASPECT OF SEX ON WHICH JUDAISM AND ALL BRANCHES OF Christianity are in firm agreement is their emphatic support of the Seventh Commandment: "Thou shalt not commit adultery!" The dictionary defines adultery as "the sexual intercourse of two persons, either of whom is married to a third person." It should be obvious by now that if marriage is to represent a complete sharing of life in mutual confidence and trust, if children are always to know the true identity of their fathers, if families are to be established and maintained on firm foundations, and if intercourse is to be one important part of a total love relationship which encompasses spiritual and emotional as well as physical bonds—husbands and wives must limit their sexual activity to each other. Indeed, in a good marriage this poses no problem. Two mature marriage partners who love each other genuinely will find

139

such fulfillment in their relationship to each other that it will be unnecessary for either to court sexual adventures elsewhere.

The Bible does not limit itself only to the terse prohibition of adultery in the Seventh Commandment. The writer of Proverbs, referring to "the evil woman" and "a harlot," warns his readers not to lust after them:

> Can a man take fire in his bosom,
> And his clothes not be burned?
> Or can one walk upon hot coals,
> And his feet not be scorched?
> So he that goeth in to his neighbor's wife;
> Whosoever toucheth her shall not go unpunished.

The prophet Hosea makes it clear that the law against adultery applies to men no less than to women. He tells his listeners they cannot expect their women to be punished for such offenses if they are guilty also:

> I will not punish your daughters when they commit harlotry,
> Nor your daughters-in-law when they commit adultery;
> For you yourselves consort with lewd women,
> And you sacrifice with harlots.

The Talmud too underscores the importance of sexual faithfulness between husband and wife. It declares: "In marriage a person reserves his partner for himself as a sacred object."[1]

Modern authorities are in agreement with this biblical and talmudic insight. We know even better than the ancients that adultery jeopardizes not only the marriage but also the integrity and mental health of the individuals involved. Thus Dr. George N. Shuster has written ". . . we are coming slowly to recognize that the psychological impact of infidelity—on the man and the woman involved, on the injured partners and particularly on the children of the married couple—is far greater than we had previously thought. Anyone who thinks that adultery, gone into however lightly and however gracefully, cannot completely shatter the life of the injured partner is terribly mistaken."[2] To which it can be added that the life of the adulterer can be no less shattered than that of the injured partner.

And Before Marriage?

While there is no disagreement among knowledgeable people about the undesirability of extra-marital intercourse or adultery, there have been some who have defended pre-marital coitus. Those who uphold the right of young men and women to experience sexual intercourse before marriage offer a variety of reasons to justify their view. The first is that *everybody's doing it.* They cite as evidence a number of studies which seem to indicate that the frequency of such experimentation has increased. They tell us, for example, that among women born about 1890, something like eighty-seven per cent were virgins at the time of their weddings; among those born after 1910, the percentage of virgins had been reduced to thirty-two per cent. Approximately half of the men born about 1890 declared themselves to be celibates on their wedding days, with only fourteen per cent of those born after 1910 placing themselves in this category. As we shall see in a moment, statistics such as these are not always as reliable as they appear to be. Even if they are, however, they would say nothing about the right or wrong of such conduct.

If seventy per cent of all drivers were found to ignore major traffic rules, the fact that they happened to be in the majority would neither excuse their behavior nor recommend it as safe procedure for the public to emulate. Cheating on an exam at school would be no more commendable ethically if done by eighty per cent of the student body than if by only twenty per cent. If scientific studies were to indicate that ninety-five per cent of the population suffers from a severe cold each winter, that would not make illness a desirable thing. So we must not exaggerate the importance of our statistics as a guide to wise behavior.

What to Believe?

We ought also to be cautious of the "tall tales" frequently told by friends—either about themselves or others. The conversation

among girls at "hen parties" and boys in the locker room is sometimes enough to make one wonder whether there is any such thing
left as pre-marital chastity. Much of this conversation, however, is
just plain boasting. Dr. William G. Cole, when he was Dean of
Freshmen at Williams College, was in a position to know. He
wrote:

> There is among very many college men widespread
> talk which would lead the casual listener to believe
> that virginity was virtually nonexistent. But most
> of this is talk of the order of the penitent who was
> cautioned by his confessor that he was not confess-
> ing but bragging . . . More careful investigation
> reveals that, in general, our college students are far
> more virtuous than they appear.[3]

Despite the sensational reports which have attracted much public
attention, sober studies on large coeducational college campuses
both before and after the Second World War disclosed that more
than half the men and women interviewed reported they had
experienced no intercourse before marriage and that two-thirds of
both sexes are opposed to such intercourse in theory.[4] What all of
this adds up to is that *far* from *everybody's doing it;* and even if
they were, distinguishing right from wrong is not a matter of
counting votes.

A second excuse sometimes given to justify intercourse before
marriage is that ethics, after all, are relative. There are societies in
which young people are encouraged to have coitus before marriage; indeed, in a few cultures a girl is not considered desirable as
a bride until after she has demonstrated her capacity to become
pregnant. While our culture prohibits adultery, among some
peoples a host is considered inhospitable if he fails to offer his
guest one of his wives as a sexual partner. Who is to say, it is
added, that our ways of judging sexual ethics are any better than
theirs?

This may at first seem sound; actually it does not hold up at all
under closer examination. To begin with, those cultures in which
pre-marital sex standards differ so widely from ours are cultures

which are more primitive than ours in nearly all respects. In addition, careful research has disclosed them to be societies in which no lasting family loyalties are created. There is, in other words, a clear correlation between our kind of sex ethics and our kind of family structure.

Another word is in order on this matter of the alleged relativity of ethics. Varying standards among different cultures may be found in areas of scientific knowledge and art as well as in standards of sex behavior. The same societies held up as examples which prove the case for ethical relativity are the very ones which lack our scientific sophistication and whose standards of music, for example, are not much higher than the beating of tom-toms and chanting of weird melodies. Would anyone want seriously to suggest that because they believe the earth to be flat, their opinion on this point is as valid as ours? Or that the beating of drums is as fine an example of music as Beethoven's Ninth Symphony? We recognize in these areas that some societies have achieved a higher level of cultural evolution than others. We do not condemn peoples or groups we perceive to be on a lower level than our own. Nor do we deny that there may be some respects in which they are more highly advanced than we, some lessons we would do well to learn from them. But neither do we lose all sense of proportion by asserting that all standards in science and music are of equal value, that there is no legitimate way of distinguishing inferior from superior levels of culture.   What is true of science and art is true of sexual conduct. The reality is that in some portions of the earth pre-marital sex standards differ from ours. This may even be the case in countries that are not primitive or uncivilized. There is valid reason to suspect that in such lands—precisely as a consequence of their sexual values and expectations—marriage and the family suffer. We shall have more to say about this at a later point.

Easy on the Boys

A third rationalization for intercourse prior to marriage refers to boys especially. It suggests that if they are permitted to get a certain amount of sexual curiosity and experimentation out of their systems while young, they will settle down to a more sober and respectable life later. A Chassidic rabbi knew how unwise this is. He said:

> Some parents believe it is permissible for their sons to sow their wild oats, so that vice may lose its allurement and they may be convinced that the experience is not worth the effort. This policy is incorrect and should be avoided. We learn this from Moses. According to the Midrash . . . the father-in-law of Moses, Jethro, persuaded Moses to allow his eldest son, Gershom, to visit the pagan temples, and attend the pagan schools, in order that he might be convinced of their worthlessness. Then, said Jethro, he will turn to the worship of the Lord out of conviction rather than tradition. The outcome, however, was that there remained in Gershom's family a tradition of the ways and allurements of paganism, and when Jonathan, his son, was in want, he readily consented to make use of this knowledge, and became a priest in the pagan temple.[5]

If it were true that sowing one's wild oats when young helped men settle down later to a more stable married life, we would expect to find less adultery among such men than among those who waited to have intercourse after marriage. In point of fact, however, the opposite is true. The research of Dr. Ira L. Reiss discloses, not surprisingly, that more men who engage in pre-marital coitus also are guilty of extra-marital infidelity than are those who abstained before marriage. This substantiates our statement a while back that men tend to take with them into marriage the patterns of sexual conduct they followed before marriage. Dr. Reiss finds the correlation easy to understand:

> These men separated sexual behavior and affection in their premarital coitus: it is therefore not difficult for them to engage in extramarital coitus purely for pleasure . . . This sort of training may well be conducive to double-standard extramarital intercourse in later years.[6]

Closely related to the foregoing is a fourth alleged justification—that men who have already experienced intercourse make better husbands than those who have not. Sometimes a girl will assert that she wants a man "who knows what it's all about" so she can learn from him. Both experience and research, however, indicate how mistaken such ideas are. Sexual experience with one girl, far from being a guarantee of success with another, may in fact make it more difficult. The sex relationship between one man and one woman is the most personal and intimate in the world. While there are, to be sure, certain general recommendations which can help every couple, there is no one pattern which is best for all. For a man to say he wants to taste of a full sex life in order later to adjust to his wife makes no more sense than to say he wants to wear clothes that please his current girl friend in order later to please his wife, or that he has decided to converse only in French, the language of the girl he is now dating, without regard for the fact that he may marry a girl who is totally ignorant of French. The preferences and tastes of the one may be altogether different from those of the other.

There is no reason to suppose that the prospects for success in marriage are at all improved by one of the partners having had more previous sexual experience than the other. As a matter of fact, the opportunity to learn together from the beginning, to taste of a wondrously new adventure for the first time, to share both successes and failures and thus grow to fulfillment—all this provides a young couple with a most promising ingredient of happiness.

Far from improving the prospect of a happy marriage, premarital sexual adventures often decrease the probability of later success, because of themselves these experiences are pathetically unsatisfactory. It is a rare couple who finds that their very first experiment with intercourse is mutually pleasurable and satisfying. Even in marriage the average couple must work for and with each other over a period of time to achieve a good adjustment. Many couples need weeks, more than a few require months, some discover that as long as a year of trial and error may be necessary before they find the answers most satisfactory to both. In marriage such loving cooperation and experimentation is possible; it even serves to draw husband and wife closer together. Before marriage many complications make a good sexual adjustment extremely improbable. Such experiences usually take place furtively, under hasty and uncongenial circumstances, accompanied by fear of discovery, guilt, and shame. A psychiatrist has described the situation accurately: "One of the miserable things about such experiences is that they are so seldom even faintly satisfactory. Much more often they are sordid and incomplete attempts which leave both partners guilty and ashamed."[7]

Maxine Davis, a knowledgeable writer of many articles and books on sex problems, has summarized very well the truth we have been trying to express in these last few paragraphs:

> Physical union before marriage is very seldom a preview of sexual love within marriage. When it is one of many promiscuous encounters, to the boy it is merely an exciting sensual episode during which he is interested only in his own satisfaction. It has no other meaning, no past, no future. It does not involve present liking or future friendship. To some boys it is comparable to gulping a long drink of water when they are thirsty. In others, especially younger boys, it may leave an after-taste of shame or disgust or worry about inadequate technique or abilities. This can affect their sexual relations for years, even for life.
>
> For a girl it is not likely to be genuinely pleasurable. A boy bent primarily on his own gratification does not behave like a bridegroom. Her feelings are her own; he does not have to care about them or live with them after they separate. He is violent and hasty, not gentle or considerate. As a result she may be frightened and repelled.
>
> This can give a false idea of what sexual experience is like within as well as outside of marriage. If she becomes promiscuous in order to have dates, a girl comes to tolerate it. She may think the sexual act is ugly and repugnant but that she is going to have to school herself to accept it when she marries in order to enjoy the companionship of a husband

she enjoys in other ways and to have the home and children she naturally wants. In that case she would never learn to participate wholeheartedly in her marital relations. This would be serious. Within marriage sexuality as part of love becomes the body's expression of love. The wife who is unable to share this unique joy because her earlier experiences had convinced her that it did not exist reduces her chances of helping to create a happy home.[8]

Final among the excuses tediously offered to justify pre-marital intercourse is the so-called double standard. For many centuries, both in Europe and this country, it was considered acceptable for men to "sow their wild oats," but women were expected to remain virgins until they were married. This duality was based on two premises which we now know to be false. The first was that only men have sexual desires, pleasures and needs. We have already discovered in an earlier chapter that this is not so; women can and should be just as active sex partners in marriage as their husbands.

The second false premise of the double-standard theory was a bit of biological ignorance. It was assumed for much of our human history on this earth that the cell from which new life develops came entirely from the male. According to this theory all that is needed for conception is the male spermatozoon and a congenial place—more or less like a nest—in which it is to be accommodated while incubating. This, obviously, gave women a status far inferior to that of men. Today we know that the two sexes are equally essential and important in the creation of new life. A baby can result only from the union of male spermatozoon with a female ovum.

Since neither excuse for a double standard is valid—since women are by nature as potentially active sexually as men and at least as important as men in the process of conception—the double standard itself must be rejected. With only the one significant difference enforced by biology—the fact that women alone can become pregnant—the same standards must apply to both sexes. Either both indulge in pre-marital intercourse or both abstain until marriage.

Even men who profess to see validity in the double standard usually apply it in a curious way. A man is likely to use it to justify sexual indulgence for himself and the girl he happens to be dating at the moment, but not for the girl who will some day be his wife. What such a man is really saying is: "I want my future wife to be a virgin but I don't care about someone else's future wife, who is my date tonight!"

Dr. Lester Kirkendall has conducted extensive research among men who experienced intercourse prior to marriage. He was particularly interested in seven men who admitted they had unsuccessfully attempted to have intercourse with their wives prior to the wedding. Here, verbatim, are the comments some of them made:

> I don't think I would have married her if she had been willing.
>
> It increased my respect for her when she refused. I have always more or less lost respect for a girl when she entered into intercourse.
>
> When a girl is too easy to make . . . I don't care for her at all. The girl who stops you is the kind I respect.[9]

It becomes apparent, then, that the double standard is less legitimate by far than some of its defenders have supposed.

In Summary

What this chapter adds up to is that, on close examination, the easy excuses given to justify intercourse before marriage are not valid. We have seen that:

—So-called statistical studies exaggerate the number of young people who experience pre-marital coitus.

—Even if it were true that *everybody's doing it,* this would be a poor basis on which to distinguish right from wrong.

—The fact that sex standards differ from one society to another does not prevent us from recognizing that some are ethically superior to others.

—Sowing wild oats early in life—far from assuring sober, responsible sex behavior later—may establish a pattern of irresponsibility which will be carried into marriage too.

—Intercourse before marriage does not improve the prospect for happiness in marriage; it may even decrease the probability of such happiness.

—The double standard is utterly fallacious. Whatever we adopt in the way of pre-marital sex ethics must be applied equally to both sexes.

In Chapter Eleven we shall try to see whether our single standard should be one of continence or indulgence.

For Instance

A. Frank and Rose have never made a good sex adjustment in the six years of their marriage. From the beginning Rose had been willing to have sex relations with him only on rare occasions, and then seldom with real satisfaction to either of them. On most occasions when Frank suggested intercourse, she begged off because of a bad headache or being too tired. Usually for several days after such an episode they would either practically ignore each other or fight aggressively.

Several times Frank had suggested going together to see a marriage counselor, but Rose refused. Now he is just about at his wit's end. The last time they had an argument over sex, he really blew up—telling Rose that he had certain needs and if she as his wife wasn't willing to meet them, he would find some other woman who would. Rose responded defiantly that he wouldn't dare, that if she ever found out he had gone to another woman she would disgrace him publicly and insist on a divorce.

> Who is justified in this dispute? What seems to be the cause of their difficulty? Would more and better sex education for either of them have helped? What can they do now to

help matters? What will be the probable effect on their marriage if Frank goes through with his threat? If he does nothing, just allowing things to go on as they have?

B. Dan has experienced full sex relations with several girls. He has never really been in love but feels confident that when the time comes he will not regret what he has done. "I feel," he has said, "that it's better for me to have had this kind of opportunity before I meet the girl I'll some day marry. After all, how could I know otherwise what intercourse is supposed to be like or whether what I have with my wife is good? If I waited, I might never know what I had missed. This way I'll have a basis of comparison."

> How valid is Dan's argument? Suppose, on the basis of the comparison he mentioned, he decided later that his sex life with his wife was not as good as his previous adventures? With how many women would he have to participate in this kind of experience before he could be satisfied? Does his reasoning sound as if it would justify such comparisons only up to the point of his marriage?

C. As Helen approaches her wedding date, scheduled for a month hence, she finds herself becoming more and more apprehensive, especially about the sexual side of marriage. She is a virgin and glad of it, but wishes she knew a little more about sex. Her parents have never really told her much; she had been too embarrassed to ask questions either of them or her married friends.

Under these circumstances she is really glad that Alvin, her groom, has had experience in such matters. She is confident she can depend upon him to teach her everything he knows. "How much more embarrassed I would be," she has thought to herself, "if neither of us knew anything. I would certainly never want Al to have intercourse with any other woman after we're married but I'm rather pleased that he already has."

> How might Helen's apprehension and embarrassment have been prevented? Is she correct in believing that it is better for Alvin to teach her what he already knows from

experience than for the two of them to learn together? Why? How valuable will his previous experience be in their marriage?

D. Since Ned entered college and joined a fraternity, he found himself deeply troubled over ideas about sex he had previously taken for granted. Judging from the conversations of his fraternity brothers, he seemed to be just about the only one in the house who was still celibate.

The young biology instructor to whom he had gone for advice encouraged him to experience intercourse. "It isn't natural," he said, "to repress your sexual urges. Wherever we look in the animal kingdom, we see that the young male begins to have intercourse as soon as he is biologically ready for it. After all, we human beings are animals too. We can't fight nature, and the need to satisfy our sexual desires is a part of nature. A man who doesn't have intercourse before marriage builds up so strong a sex need that his wife will never be able to satisfy him. As a result, he is less likely to remain faithful after marriage than if he had indulged. So my advice to you is to stop trying to be the exception that proves the rule."

How good was this advice? Why? Was the instructor correct in his comparison of men and animals? Is it true that satisfaction of our sexual desires is a part of nature? Were any factors of importance omitted by the instructor? Is it true that abstinence before marriage decreases the probability of faithfulness after marriage?

E. "The trouble with your ideas regarding a single standard is that they assume the two sexes are the same." This was Lanny's opening comment to the author of this book.

"Actually," he continued, "men and women are not the same in their sex needs. Those of men are stronger by far. Sure, some women may develop active sex lives after they are married, but they can take or leave sex before marriage. A man needs to release his sexual tension before marriage; a woman doesn't. So long as this is true, it doesn't make sense to talk about a single standard for both. It's a lot better for a man to get the release he needs through intercourse than by masturbating."

Is Lanny right or wrong? Are there differences in sex needs and desires between men and women? Is it true that premarital intercourse is preferable to masturbation? Why? If you were the author, how would you have answered Lanny?

Chapter ELEVEN

DOES IT REALLY MAKE A DIFFERENCE?

BY EXPOSING THE SHABBINESS OF THE USUAL EXCUSES USED TO justify intercourse before marriage, Chapter Ten implied that the single standard of sex conduct for unmarried men and women should be one of chastity. In this chapter we propose to consider more explicit reasons for this implication. Among them are two very old ones. Though they are not the best reasons—the best we shall come to later—it would nonetheless be both foolish and dangerous to deny them. The first is the elementary biological fact that coitus leads to pregnancy both before and after marriage. The ovum and spermatozoon do not know whether or not their respective hosts are married!

Young people sometimes suppose they can avoid the danger of pregnancy by utilizing a birth control technique. They need to remember that (a) no such method is one hundred per cent sure, that (b) the more reliable of them require the cooperation and direction of a competent physician, and that (c) the percentage of failure is much larger among the unmarried than among the married. Anyone who doubts the continuing danger of pregnancy, despite our knowledge of contraception, need only study the figures reporting the number of children born to unmarried mothers in the United States. In doing so, moreover, it should be remembered that these represent only the number that is known; there have undoubtedly been many more that were never reported.

1938— 87,900
1949—133,200
1957—201,700
1960—224,000

The number of children born to unmarried teen-age mothers rose from 8.4 per thousand in 1940 to sixteen per thousand in 1961. In the twenty to twenty-five age group the number rose during the same time span from 11.2 to 41.2 per thousand.[1]

The statistics on abortion are pertinent here too. Some unmarried girls who discover they are pregnant foolishly resort to an illegal attempt to terminate their pregnancy. We have already mentioned the grave dangers attendant upon such attempts. It was estimated as long ago as 1950 that between 1,000,000 and 1,800,000 abortions took place in the United States annually. Though we have no way of knowing how many of these were medically authorized and how many represented unmarried girls, there can be no doubt that the latter constituted a substantial portion of the total figure. They too must be counted among the casualties of pre-marital intercourse.

Please observe that nowhere in this discussion have we used the term *illegitimate children*. There is no such thing as an illegitimate child—only illegitimate parents. A child does not ask to be born. It is innocent and blameless, no matter what the circumstances of its conception. True, it is likely to suffer in many ways if born to unmarried parents—or even if born to parents who married only under duress due to pregnancy. But no guilt should ever be ascribed to the child himself.

In the light of the evidence presented here, let no one be so foolish as to suppose that the danger of an unwanted pregnancy is no longer a factor to be considered in pre-marital sex encounters. Any rabbi or physician can testify from his own professional experience to the agony experienced by two unmarried young people who discover that, despite their most careful calculations, they have conceived a new life. What should be the most sacred and exalted moment in human experience becomes cheap and besmudged. Incalculable anguish is suffered by the couple, as well as by their parents. If they marry, friends lift suspicious eyebrows when their first child appears in less than nine months. Sometimes a shadow of guilt and remorse hovers permanently over a marriage which might otherwise have been a wonderful relationship. Not even this is the whole story. The anguish suffered by a girl who eventually learns that she is not pregnant—but who is horrified by a tardy menstrual period, knowing that she has had intercourse and *could be* pregnant—is not to be discounted lightly. The one and only sure way for an unmarried girl to prevent pregnancy is to avoid intercourse or any other experience which could place male sperm in or near her vagina.

Pathetic echoes of the enduring tragedy and heartache which afflict the parents of an unmarried pregnant girl are evident in the following excerpts from a letter published in *The Saturday Review* of August 15, 1964. In response to an article on "Campus Mores," published in an earlier issue of the magazine, a distraught father wrote the following:

> To all those college students, high school students, teen agers, and others who want to indulge in sexual intercourse without marriage I would propound this question and demand an answer: "Are you personally prepared to assume full responsibility for pregnancies, illegitimate births, or physical or psychological damage that may result to you or your sexual partner because of these acts and to relieve your parents and others of the burden of such results?" . . . As the father of a daughter who made a "mistake" in college, gave the child for adoption, underwent psychiatric treatment for two years, and then had to go back to school to try to make some kind of new life, and who necessarily

Does It Really Make a Difference? 155

threw much of the burden on her family. I would say that sexual "freedom" is first of all a matter of responsibility and the ability and willingness to assume it. To those who have not the willingness and ability to assume responsibility, the freedom should be denied. In general, I would say that sexual intercourse is for responsible men and women and not for irresponsible boys and girls. . . .

This letter is a testimony of a deep and harsh experience that has not ended after eight years and may never be ended, for there is little hope that my beautiful daughter will ever be anything like what she might have been.

Another Danger

The second old-fashioned reason which recommends chastity is the possibility of contracting venereal diseases. These are principally two in number: syphilis and gonorrhea. They are transmitted from one person to another almost always through intercourse and are among the most dreaded of all diseases known to man. In both sexes they can result in blindness, in deformed children, in paralysis and mental deterioration. In order to secure a marriage license it is now necessary in most states first to have one's blood tested to make sure neither party suffers from a venereal disease. But there is no way in the world of insuring that a partner in pre-marital coitus is free from infection.

Here again, there are some who minimize the danger, saying that we now have drugs which can control and even cure these diseases. Though we do in fact have such medication, successful cures depend on early diagnosis and treatment. Most parties to a pre-marital sex adventure are understandably not anxious to disclose this fact, even to a physician. As a result, in many cases the disease is not recognized until early treatment is impossible.

Unfortunately, the statistics here are as devastating as they were in the case of unwanted pregnancies. An article in the *New York Times* of May 6, 1962, written by Dr. Howard Rusk, bears the alarming heading—*Syphilis Cases Rise*. It reads in part as follows:

The battle against venereal disease is far from won even with such available allies as penicillin and other new therapeutic tools.

The 18,781 reported cases of infectious syphilis in the United States in the fiscal year 1961 was not only double the 1960 rate but triple the 1959 rate and was the greatest number reported since 1950. . . .

Even more shocking than the marked increase in infectious syphilis is the fact that the greatest increase has been among young persons. The disease increased fifty-nine percent in the fifteen to nineteen year age group and seventy-three percent in the twenty to twenty-four year age group between 1959 and 1960.

Later in the same article Dr. Rusk attributed this frightening situation to, among other things, "lowering of moral standards" and "inadequate parental control of teen-agers."

The trend reported by Dr. Rusk in 1962 has continued. On December 13, 1964, the *New York Times* reported more recent statistics disclosed by government health authorities. They showed that in the year ending in June 1963, known cases of infectious syphilis totaled 22,733, while those of gonorrhea came to 290,603. But the situation is even worse than the alarming figures indicate. The *Times* went on to say:

The United States Public Health Service says the statistics, as bad as they are, do not tell the whole story.

They say that . . . the actual number, including hidden, unreported cases, is probably vastly higher.

The United States Public Health Service estimated the true total of syphilis cases for the year to be about 200,000, of gonorrhea about 290,600. Again, the most alarming increases were among teen-agers. Between 1956 and 1963 reported cases of new syphilis among persons under the age of twenty rose more than two hundred per cent!

Does It Really Make a Difference? 157

You may at some time hear the convenient and apparently comforting rationalization that veneral diseases are a major threat only in the lower socio-economic classes or among certain racial groups. Government studies show this to be untrue. Experts of the United States Public Health Service assure us that the horrifying increase disclosed in 1964 "is not confined to any race, sex, socio-economic group, or geographic area," that it has occurred quite generally throughout the nation.

Ignoring such unpleasant facts as these may cater to one's whims of the moment. The possible price to be paid—either in an unwanted pregnancy or a dread disease or both—makes for a very bad bargain. We said at the outset of this section that these two old-fashioned reasons for chastity are not the best. They are both obviously based on fear. In our sex lives, as in all other areas of human experience, conduct based on positive motivations is far preferable to that based on fear. Let us turn, then, to positive reasons for recommending pre-marital chastity.

Better Reasons

The most persuasive and important argument for delaying sexual intercourse until after marriage springs from what has already been said about the unique role of sex in human life as compared to animal life. We have already seen that among all sub-human forms of life, sex is a purely physical and, for the most part, transitory experience. A male dog happens upon a female dog which is "in heat," which means to say, is ovulating and therefore amenable to advances by the male. They proceed to have intercourse—physically in much the same manner and with bodily sensations similar to ours. The male having satisfied his desires, they go their separate ways, unaware of any permanent consequences resulting from this momentary act. The next time either of them indulges in intercourse, it is most likely to be with a different partner and is again a passing incident.

There are differences, however, even among various species of animals. In their sexual behavior—as in many other areas of conduct—some animals show the earliest beginnings of characteristics which are destined to emerge fully on the later human level of evolution. Thus, there are a few species of animal life which seem to anticipate the human love relationship of one-to-one. The bald eagle and wild goose both mate for life with only one member of the opposite sex. The wolf—ironically enough in view of our use of his name to designate a particular kind of human male—mates with only one female during her life span and will take a second mate only upon the death of the first. While these are interesting anticipations of humanity, it must be remembered that even in these instances of animal "monogamy," the relationship is still entirely of a physical nature.

Some human beings live their sex lives on a level not too different from what has just been described. But we can scarcely call their conduct in this respect truly human. It is only animal behavior with a somewhat greater comprehension of the consequences. To be genuinely human, our sex relations must be on both physical and spiritual levels. The physical sensations of intercourse must be tied in with a whole host of mental, emotional and spiritual components—all of which together add up to the experience of love.

Sex in animal life may be represented in this way:

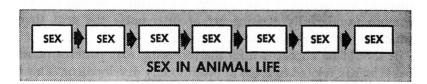

SEX IN ANIMAL LIFE

Each experience of intercourse is on the same level as the last, each isolated from the experience preceding and following it.

Julian Huxley, the great British biologist, has called our attention to several startling illustrations of the fact that among animals sexual intercourse is a transitory and purely physical experience. He has written:

> . . . many birds will attempt to mate with a stuffed dead female as readily as with a real live one—provided that it is set up in a certain pose; and the sperm for artificial insemination in cattle and

horses can be obtained because the mating urge of bulls and stallions is aroused by suitable dummies as well as by live cows or mares.[2]

Sex in human life may be symbolized as follows:

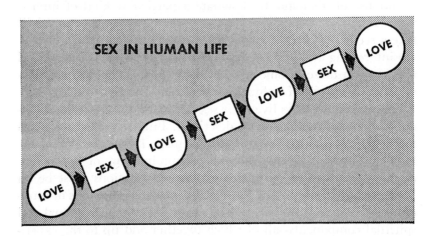

It is love which makes intercourse a human rather than just an animal experience. Each act of intercourse then increases the quantity and quality of love between the partners, leading them to a more wonderfully exciting act of intercourse the next time, which in turn increases love still further.

It should be apparent from the foregoing that patterns of sex behavior are related to levels of evolutionary development. This is true not only with reference to the differences between animal and human conduct, but also among human beings themselves.

We do not all stand on the same level of evolutionary development. Some human beings are still relatively close to the animal kingdom. Others are so highly developed in refinement, intelligence, ethical values and sensitivity as to be on what might be called the "growing edge" of evolutionary development—pointing the way, as it were, to the next stage of the process. It would appear that a superior level of pre-marital sex behavior goes along with other kinds of superiority. Certain studies have disclosed, for example, that among male high school graduates there are eight times as many celibates before marriage as among grade school graduates, while among college graduates there are sixteen times as many.[3]

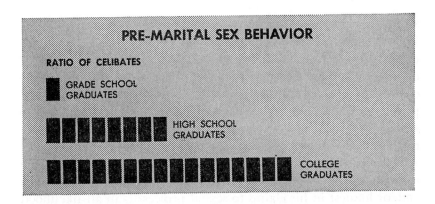

PRE-MARITAL SEX BEHAVIOR

RATIO OF CELIBATES

GRADE SCHOOL GRADUATES

HIGH SCHOOL GRADUATES

COLLEGE GRADUATES

Varying levels of pre-marital sexual conduct are also correlated with emotional maturity. In our earlier discussion of maturity we mentioned as one of its most distinctive traits the ability to defer a momentary pleasure in preference to a greater gain in the future. In no area is this truer than sex. It is sometimes erroneously supposed that the young person who indulges in intercourse at an early age is sexually more mature than one who abstains. Nothing could be more deceptive. Psychologists are agreed that it is apt to be precisely the boy or girl who is least mature and secure who seeks sexual adventures as a means of falsely reassuring himself! One scholar summarizes his investigation of sexual conduct among junior and senior high school students as follows:

> First, teen-agers who trust themselves and their ability to contribute to others and who have learned to rely on others socially and emotionally are least likely to be involved in irresponsible sexual activity. . . .

> Second, teen-agers who have learned to be comfortable in their appropriate sex roles (boys who like being boys and wish to be men, and girls who like being girls and wish to be women) are least likely to be involved in activities leading to indiscriminate sexuality. . . .

Third, both boys and girls have a need to discuss serious problems with adults who they feel can be helpful—that is to say, trusted.[4]

Studies conducted by two British Army psychiatrists during World War II substantiate these conclusions. They evaluated the maturity of two hundred venereal disease patients, compared to that of eighty-seven others who were hospitalized for illness having no connection with sex conduct. Fifty-nine per cent of the venereal patients proved to be "immature personality types," contrasted to nineteen per cent of the others. Only eleven per cent of the venereally infected men were judged to be "mature personality types," as against sixty-two per cent of the others![5] Clearly, then, the individual who seems to be boldest in his sex behavior patterns and/or loudest in his claims to sexual prowess is in all likelihood seeking frantically to convince himself of a security which isn't there.

In Chapter Ten we found that pre-marital intercourse does not aid in making a good marriage, that in fact it may be a serious obstacle. We are now ready to add, more positively, that chastity before marriage can greatly enhance our happiness in marriage. To indulge in pre-marital intercourse is to isolate sexual union from all the other factors which go with it in love. It is highly questionable whether one can experience sex for a number of years on a purely physical basis—entirely divorced from feelings of tenderness and lasting love—then suddenly pull a switch, as it were, after which one participates in the same behavior from a spiritual point of view too. The earliest experiences a man or woman has with coitus are likely to establish an atmosphere and attitude which will surround all subsequent experiences for that person.

A psychiatrist and a writer who collaborated a few years back on a book combining the insights of psychiatry and religion wrote this:

> Sexual intercourse is but one item in a total human relationship and it provides emotional fulfillment only as it is an expression of mature love between a man and a woman in marriage. Advice that overlooks this is likely to have dangerous results.[6]

Similar advice has been given by another physician, Dr. Max Levin, Clinical Professor of Neurology at the New York Medical College:

> Sex is more than a mechanism for procreation, and it is more than an avenue for sensual gratification. It is a function that promotes the growth of character. It is in the realm of sex that people reveal most clearly their real character and the degree of their emotional maturity. The behavior of man and wife in the sex act is the most sensitive index of their capacity to give, of their refusal to receive satisfaction unless they also give it.[7]

The boy who indulges in full sex expression with several girls grows accustomed to thinking primarily of himself and his own gratification. He is much more likely to concentrate on what he can obtain out of the experience for himself than on how he can provide satisfaction and pleasure also for his partner. And he is apt to take this concentration on himself with him into the sexual side of his marriage. In the words of one who has carefully studied every aspect of pre-marital coitus, under these circumstances "intercourse is an episode, rather than a relationship."[8] One wife, whose husband had had many adventures with prostitutes, commented: "About twice a week he takes me and uses me." A husband who had experienced full sex relations with other girls before his marriage quoted his wife as complaining that "I treat her like a girl in the back seat of a car."[9]

The husband and wife who begin their experience with intercourse together are sharing the whole of life and love. They are building a sturdy, integrated structure from the foundation up, rather than trying to piece together and repair various aspects of love which previously existed in isolation. They are not forced to unlearn old associations and habits which detract from the fulness of their love. The physical pleasure and joy of their intercourse is both a consequence and a cause of their emotional and spiritual relationship. Their life together is a whole, not a patchwork of parts.

In short, those who would insure themselves the greatest chance for happiness and success in marriage stand to lose by pre-marital adventures and to gain by waiting. This, in the last analysis, is the best reason to wait. Not because we may be punished if we indulge in intercourse before marriage—though it is true that we may be— but because there is so much happiness to be obtained if we earn it.

Perhaps one reason for the increase in pre-marital intercourse which we noted earlier is that too much emphasis has been put on the negative reasons for continence and not enough on the *positive reasons*. Thus, a well-known psychiatrist and psychologist, (husband and wife, by the way!) after observing how "shallow and incomplete" purely physical sexual intercourse is and how glorious and wonderful it can be when married partners are united both physically and spiritually, go on to say:

> If parents approach sex education from such a standpoint, there is no problem in advocating moral behavior in the premarital years. It would not be advocated because of the dangers of violating the code, but because of the advantages of adhering to it—the assurance of a better marriage.[10]

Judaism has always recognized that the sex life of human beings should be different from that of animals. When Genesis says that man was created in the image of God, this means that every one of us is sacred, that no one is entitled to *use* another person as though he were only an impersonal object. To treat another person merely as a device by which to gratify one's own desires is to defile God's image, both in the other person and in oneself.

The great Jewish philosopher, Martin Buber, has introduced us to the distinction in human relations between I-It and I-Thou. I-It means treating another person as if he or she were only a thing. If I move a chair aside because it stands in my way, there is an I-It relationship between the chair and myself. It makes no difference to the chair where it is placed or how many times it is moved. But if I rudely bump into you because you happen to be in my way, it does make a difference to you. You are a human being, with feelings, fears, hopes and needs very much like mine. I have no right to use you for my own purposes. I must relate myself to you on an I-Thou basis. If not, I act as if only I were created in God's image, not you.

This is true in all our relationships with other people. It is especially true in our sex relationships. When one person exploits another only for the gratification of his own sexual desires or to inflate his own ego, he has forgotten one of the most precious principles of Judaism.

Only Theory?

Marriage is one of many areas in which the ancient wisdom of Judaism and ethics is now being confirmed by scientific studies. Many experts who have devoted years to careful study of the factors which lead to a happy marriage have concluded that premarital chastity is one of them. Dr. James A. Peterson summarizes "all of the careful studies of the way premarital sexual experience influences marital success." He says: "All of them, without exception, indicate that those marriages which are contracted between couples who did not have premarital sex are more successful than those who did."[11]

Dr. Peterson is far from the only one to reach this conclusion. Drs. Rose and Abraham Franzblau, whom we have already quoted in another connection, have discovered how often couples who indulge in intercourse before marriage later feel cheated.

> It is a strange thing that when married couples look back, in the psychiatrist's office, at their premarital sex, they often regret it and wish they had waited. They stress the importance of continence to their children. The girl may carry guilt feelings into her marriage; she may feel robbed of the excitement of her honeymoon, which becomes something of a sham after premarital sex; and she may resent having been deceived into it by her husband, who looks smaller in stature to her because he could not control his desires and wait, and who did not love her enough to protect her from her own desires.
>
> The man may also regret losing some of the thrill of the honeymoon, and may be wracked with the classical perplexity and doubt of the husband in literature and drama, who disguises himself as a lover and woos his own wife, to test her fidelity. Since the wife was weak and yielded to his blandish-

ments before marriage, had she not perhaps yielded likewise to others before him?

Perhaps there is something, after all, to the great store which has been placed on virginity down through the ages.[12]

We hate to bore you with too many quotations, but this is a factor of such importance in the making of a happy marriage that you should know how numerous experts have come to feel about it. Their observations, for the most part, are based on careful, sober, scientific study of many marriages. Thus Drs. Ernest W. Burgess and Paul Wallin write that their research supports "the conclusion that husbands and wives with no experience of premarital intercourse have the higher probability of marital success, whereas couples in which husband or wife had premarital relations with spouse and others have the lower probability."[13]

Dr. Abraham Stone, pioneer physician in the field of marriage counseling, wrapped up the conclusions of his long career in these words:

> Considerable clinical experience and contact with young people has impressed me with the fact that indiscriminate sexual relations endanger the wholesomeness and balance of one's personal and social life. In spite of our changing values, it seems to me that a lasting union of one man with one woman is still the most ideal form of human sex relationship.[14]

The considered judgment of other scholars substantially agrees. For example—

> —Dr. Lewis M. Terman:
> One's chances of marital happiness are at present favored by the selection of a mate who has not had intercourse with any other person.[15]

> —Institute of Family Relations in California:
> . . . the greatest proportion of happy marriages are among couples both of whom were virgins on their wedding day.

—Dr. Clarence Leuba:

Investigations of happiness in marriage indicate that those who were virgins at the time of marriage or who had had intercourse only with the person they eventually married were happier on the average than those who did not fall in either of these two categories.[16]

The theme of this chapter and the preceding one should not be misunderstood. We have claimed neither that every person who participates in pre-marital sex relations is doomed to an unhappy marriage nor that each one who refrains from such pre-marital experience is guaranteed a happy marriage. What we have asserted—and what experience confirms—is that sexual adjustment is one of the most important, and at the same time one of the most delicate, balances on which successful marriage depends. The couple who have both been continent before marriage have clearly the better chance to achieve such success.

In Summary

We have seen, then, that there are both negative and positive factors which recommend chastity before marriage. In the former category is the danger of pregnancy and of contracting a horrible disease. No couple that has fallen prey to either of these dread possibilities would advise their friends—or, in later years, their children—to follow their precedent.

The positive and very much more important motivation for chastity is that it helps achieve a happier marriage. We cannot have it both ways. We cannot enjoy the purely physical, animal pleasures of pre-marital sexual indulgence and also achieve later the highest possible human level of sex life and love. There is a price to be paid for every form of enjoyment or fun. In every important choice we gain something and lose something. Accurate knowledge of human nature and of mankind's experience through history leads to the conclusion that what we stand to gain through chastity is far greater than any temporary loss.

For Instance

A. Leon agrees that there is no justification for the double standard in sex behavior. Yet he disagrees with our discussion in this chapter. It is his contention that the single standard for both sexes should be a permissive one; that is to say, both men and women should be allowed to have whatever sex affairs they wish before marriage. He has, as a matter of fact, been urging this on his current girl friend. He says that despite the lack of real love between them, they both feel physically aroused when they are together and he sees no reason why they should not meet each other's needs. Since neither of them has had intercourse before, there need be no fear of disease. Since they are both intelligent college graduates, they should be able to protect the girl against pregnancy. He concedes frankly that the two of them do not have enough in common culturally or emotionally to make marriage reasonable, but to him this is no reason they shouldn't give each other pleasure for the time being in the one area they do seem to share.

> How intelligent is Leon's attitude? What are some of the possible or even probable consequences if his girl agrees? Which is preferable: a double standard, or a single standard such as Leon suggests? Why? Would he and his girl be more or less likely to marry each other if she acceded? What effect would the course of action he is urging have on a future marriage of either of them to someone else?

B. Alfred and Lois have been dating for about six months. From the beginning there has been a strong attraction between them, but they have never given serious consideration to marriage. For one thing, Alfred is a first-year student in medical school, with many more years of education and training before he can consider supporting a wife. Lois, who is a college junior, has planned to do graduate study in social work for the next few years.

For some time now they have been having intercourse. Lois has been worried since missing her last menstrual period. Yesterday she went to the doctor, who told her she is pregnant. When she told this to Alfred last night, he was shocked beyond belief. Neither of them slept at all that night; today they both skipped classes and are trying to settle on a solution.

What shall they do? Alfred already knows enough about medicine to know the risk involved in an abortion. Both of them are aware of the moral question involved in abortion. Neither of their families is in a financial position to offer them help; besides, Alfred is sure his parents would disown him if they knew, and Lois fears that her father would throw her out of the house.

> What alternatives are there for Alfred and Lois? Consider the probable results of each alternative and decide what you would recommend. If you were their rabbi and they came to you for advice, what would you tell them? To whom else should they speak? Should they get married? Why?

C. Judging from the conversation of his friends, Martin seems to be the only boy in the crowd who has not yet experienced intercourse. For some time now two of them have been urging him to go with them to a house of prostitution. Their argument is that this way no one gets hurt. There is no worry about having to marry a girl one doesn't love, no fear of giving a girl the impression that you want to become involved with her, and no danger of contracting a venereal disease because certainly professional prostitutes know how to protect their own health. His friends are sure, as a matter of fact, that these girls get regular medical examinations.

> How sure can Martin be that he is the only celibate among his friends? If he is, who is more mature—he or they? Who is more a man? How valid is each of the arguments given to Martin by his two friends? What other factors, not mentioned by them, should he take into consideration? Why?

D. Vivian and Arnold have been engaged for six months. During their courtship and the early weeks of their engagement, while they indulged in petting, they abstained from intercourse. About a month after Arnold had given her a ring, however, they did have intercourse three times. Vivian felt very guilty about it, so much that she insisted that it stop. She was so determined that she refused even to permit further petting, lest they find themselves unable to control themselves.

Since the change in Vivian, Arnold has been furious. They have had many arguments, in which he has insisted that he can't stand spending so much time in close contact with Vivian without fulfilling his sexual needs. Seeing how disagreeable the tension makes him, she has consented to his stopping at a prostitute's before coming to spend an evening with her. This seems to release his tension, and now they don't quarrel so much.

> What do you think of their solution? Is it a good way to handle the tension in Arnold? Why? Can you think of a better solution? What effect will this behavior have on their marriage? Will it increase or decrease the probability of Arnold's being faithful to Vivian after they are married?

Chapter TWELVE

BACK TO PREPARATION

EVEN AMONG THOSE WHO AGREE WITH THE CONCLUSIONS OF OUR
last two chapters, some will wish to raise a further question.

Granted that promiscuous sexual relations are harmful to the
individual and his marriage, how about intercourse between
couples who are engaged and whose wedding date may already
have been set? The Talmud would make no exception even of
these. Referring to the fact that if a cup of wine has already been
tasted, it is too late to pronounce a blessing over it, the passage we
have in mind reads: "A woman is like the cup of blessing: if one
has tasted it, it becomes faulty."[1]

It cannot be honestly denied that an engaged couple poses a
problem somewhat different from that of casual encounters. Still,
if we retrace for a moment some of the reasons which recommend
pre-marital chastity in general, it will become apparent that for

171

the most part they apply also to the engaged couple. The danger of pregnancy, for example, still exists. The most favorable circumstances for a good sexual adjustment on the basis of confident, uninterrupted privacy is still lacking. The early association of intercourse with furtiveness and guilt is still a risk. And there is always the very real, sometimes corroding and destructive suspicion: *if with me, with how many others before?*

It should also be remembered that engagements are often broken. According to one estimate, half the engagements announced in the United States are terminated short of marriage. The writer has more than once had a wedding ceremony, at which he had been scheduled to officiate, cancelled only a few days beforehand, after all arrangements had been made and the invitations sent.

Indeed, it may be that intercourse before the wedding increases the probability of a broken engagement. We can only speculate about this, but we know that the guilt resulting from pre-or-extramarital coitus can often tip the delicate balance from love to hate. There is an example of this in the Bible. In the book of Second Samuel we are told that King David's son Amnon felt so passionate a desire for his half-sister Tamar that he conspired to be alone with her and begged her to have sexual relations with him. When she refused, he forced her with his greater strength. No sooner had he accomplished his desires than we read: "Then Amnon hated her with exceeding great hatred; for the hatred wherewith he hated her was greater than the love wherewith he had loved her." The writer of this tale possessed profound psychological insight. He knew that often a person projects his own guilt after such an experience onto his partner, as a result of which he hates her (or him) bitterly.

While it is true that some engagements which might otherwise have endured may be terminated because of premature sex relations, in other cases intercourse may preserve an engagement which would have been better broken. Two people who have gone "all the way" may feel a combination of guilt and of responsibility toward each other which prevents them from acting when their engagement brings them to the realization that the prognosis for their marriage is not hopeful.

There is also reason to believe that the correlation referred to between pre-marital abstinence and success in marriage applies to the engagement period too. Burgess and Wallin have devised a scale by which to measure the success of engagements. They have concluded, as a result of much research, that "the engagement success scores of persons who had intercourse tend to be lower than the scores of those who were continent."[2] Dr. Max Levin, whom we quoted in Chapter Eleven, has addressed himself also to the problem of the engaged couple:

> There are sincere and high-minded young people who . . . see no reason to wait for the wedding night, and they wonder why they can't start their relations now—a kind of buy now, pay later program. But this, too, is a mistake.
>
> There are cases where intercourse before the wedding leads to trouble. The bridegroom, sometimes as early as the honeymoon, begins to feel a certain contempt for his bride. He thinks of the golden days when he courted her, and recalls with a feeling of shock that he didn't find it too hard to induce her to go to bed with him. The bride, too, is filled with contempt—contempt for herself. She gave in too easily to her lover's demands. She begins to hate him, feeling that he had taken unfair advantage of her ardent nature and her love for him. These destructive emotions grow, like a blister on the toe that turns into sepsis, and the once happy couple, now embittered, begin to wonder how they ever got the idea that they were meant for each other.
>
> The safest course for an engaged couple is to wait until they are married. A young man who respects his fiancee will not pressure her to go to bed with him. And she in turn will understand that his self-restraint is a sign of his respect and devotion, and she will love him all the more.
>
> Investment means putting money aside for future growth. Instead of buying a new car, you buy common stocks. You sacrifice current satisfaction for future profit. The richest investment a man can make is self-restraint during the time of his court-

ship. It will pay off in dividends far beyond what he will ever get from the finest blue chips. He will gain a happier and more loving wife, and a happier wife means a happier husband and children.[3]

All in all, then, the wisest course of conduct is for couples who have waited for each other up to and through their period of engagement to wait a bit longer for their wedding. This is not only a more mature choice; it is also the one best calculated to bring them happiness in their marriage.

How Far Is Enough?

One of the most perplexing, and at times painful problems faced by young people today is that of necking and petting. For most readers of this book it is a more immediate and vexing issue than some of those we have already discussed, which you may not actually face for some time to come. Chronologically, it may have made better sense to discuss petting and other problems of dating at an earlier point in this volume. However, we have purposely waited because of our conviction that these matters assume their greatest importance in connection with the total role of sex in marriage.

A variety of definitions of petting have been offered. One of the oldest is that necking refers to anything above the neck, petting to everything below. Most of us, when we use the word petting, refer to any fondling by boys and girls of those portions of their respective bodies which are sexually exciting.

Petting serves an important purpose in nature's scheme of things. It is meant to be the prelude and preparation for intercourse. One of the tragedies of our culture is that so much petting occurs before marriage and so little occurs afterward. For petting is nature's preface to full sexual relations; it is the way in which husbands and wives can make sure that both are ready for intercourse. When the prelude is indulged in by an unmarried couple, one of two things must result. Either they stop just short of the climax, after having excited each other passionately, thus increasing the tension intolerably; or they go farther than they should, with consequences we have already discussed.

It is almost unfair of our society to blame young people for what seems to be an increase in petting. They are given more freedom and temptation than some of them can control. Newspapers, magazines, television, movies, sex appeal in advertising—all these stimulate the sexual desires of high school and college students far beyond anything experienced a generation ago by their parents. The automobile and the demise of the chaperone have conspired to open up opportunities which are difficult to resist. But if the opportunities are greater than they once were, so is the danger.

The most important thing to remember is that petting is dynamite. Once begun, it quickly builds into an uncontrollable crescendo. The person who pets with the idea of seeing how far he can go before stopping is no wiser than someone who gambles on how far down he can allow a dynamite fuse to burn before extinguishing it. The time to control petting is very near its starting point; the longer it continues, the harder it will be to stop. Every individual in the world—with no exception!—has his or her point of no return, and no one knows in advance just where that point may be. A substantial proportion of those who go all the way, perhaps producing a pregnancy, say afterward that they had no intention of indulging in intercourse. They were just petting, confident they could stop in time, and before they knew what had happened it was too late.

Is it necessary for girls to neck or pet in order to be popular? Whenever students of high schools and colleges have been given an opportunity to answer that question, significant majorities have responded in the negative. To put the matter as plainly and bluntly as possible, the kind of popularity a girl can purchase through petting just isn't worth having. Evelyn Millis Duvall expresses this truth very well: "If one wants to be popular as a *petter,* one must pet in order to be eligible. But if one would rather be popular as a *person,* promiscuous petting is a decided handicap."[4]

Some unmarried couples have fallen into the habit of petting to the point where each has an orgasm without actual coitus. This is inadvisable for several reasons. First, the resultant guilt can be almost as uncomfortable and destructive as it is when intercourse has been experienced. Second, we have already indicated that pregnancy is possible even without the penis being placed in the vagina; all that is needed is for sperm to be deposited near the vaginal opening. Third, our remark in the early part of this chapter, about engaged couples who feel compelled by conscience to marry despite grave doubt by one or both, applies here too. Couples whose petting has proceeded to this point may also feel an obligation not to terminate a relationship which would better have been broken. Fourth and finally, developing the habit of gaining their satisfaction in this manner can be a serious obstacle to developing a more gratifying kind of orgasm for both after marriage.

The wise adolescent will decide long in advance of temptation just how far he or she intends to go and will then stick to that decision with stalwart stubbornness! The middle of a raging blizzard is no time to check on whether the storm windows are up. An ounce of prevention . . . but then you know how that ends, don't you? The wise engaged couple will determine policy in advance, discussing their values in sex conduct, how far they are both willing to go and at what point they are determined—for the sake of greater happiness later—to stop. Then they will be in a position to fortify and help each other.

While both sexes share the responsibility for self-control, more often than not it will be the girl who turns on the stop-light. Nature has given her the advantage in this respect. In the first place, she is slower to become aroused sexually than is the boy; hence she will normally still be this side of her point of no return after he has passed his. Secondly, she has more to lose: both can lose their self-respect, both can jeopardize the success of their marriage, but only she can become pregnant.

This must not be interpreted to mean that girls bear the entire responsibility for pre-marital sexual conduct. A boy who respects himself and his date, who wishes to increase the likelihood of eventual happiness in marriage for both of them, will refrain from forcing the issue to the point where everything depends on the girl. The responsibility should be shared equally. But if he should fail to assume his proper portion of the obligation, she may have to act for both.

In addition to establishing good ground-rules in advance, it is wise to keep the social setting conducive to maintaining one's resolutions. Dating with another couple or two will reduce the temptations which are more likely to develop when you and your date are alone. Drinking is never a help for self-control. It is not true—as some have suggested—that alcohol increases one's sexual desires; it is true, however, that it decreases one's control over his own impulses and emotions. The person who sincerely wants to live a long, healthy life doesn't go about balancing on one foot at the edge of a skyscraper. He may get away with it, but then again, he may not!

Too Late?

One final word before leaving this subject. We hope these last three chapters have reached you in time to prevent any serious or crippling mistake. But suppose they haven't? Suppose you have already indulged in a kind of sex behavior which you now realize was unhealthy? Does that mean it is too late for you to start planning for a wholesome and happy marriage? No, not at all. Judaism has always taught the importance of forgiveness and atonement. But it is not a cheap forgiveness or an easy atonement which our faith finds acceptable. We have been told for many centuries that in order to be forgiven it is necessary to acknowledge humbly one's error or sin, then to repair any damage that may have been caused to another, then to resolve firmly that the error once made will henceforth be avoided. And our rabbis add that the only real test of valid atonement is whether, when confronted by the same temptation again, one is able to resist.

If you have already made a mistake, the important thing is to learn from it and to improve. Atonement and forgiveness mean trying to find out *why* the mistake was committed, in order that next time it may be corrected. Such genuine atonement and improvement are far more likely if there is some person older than yourself whom you can trust enough to share the error that troubles you. Of one thing you may be sure: anyone who really loves you will love you no less after discovering that you are not perfect. If you are fortunate in your marriage, some day your husband or wife will give you this kind of help. Meanwhile it can be a parent or an older, wiser friend.

Sex is power. Like every kind of power, it can be used for tremendous good or misused for incalculable harm. You are the only one in the world who can make that choice for yourself. You and your future mate are the ones who will benefit most delightfully if you choose wisely, and who will suffer most painfully if you do not. Many years ago, Dr. Evelyn Millis Duvall, whose wise words about sex and marriage we have already had occasion to quote, wrote the following beautiful and significant passage:

> Sex is a part of life. It can be fine and full and very beautiful. It can be painful, restricting, and shameful. Like every other source of power, it must be harnessed or it runs wild and becomes destructive. Electricity wired into your home will light your house, cook your meals, warm your feet, and perform all kinds of miracles. Left unleashed as lightning, it can destroy everything you care about in one burning holocaust. So it is with sex. It can be the basis of the fullest friendships, the finest love, the happiest marriage, and the supreme satisfaction of home and parenthood. Or it can, if left to run wild, hurt and destroy and leave forever scarred all that you hold dear.
>
> Your sex life is yours to choose. More than ever before in history young people are given the freedom to work out their own behavior and to run their own lives. Your sex worries, your difficulties with sex are yours to work out with all the help that modern science and religion can offer. Your fulfillment of the sex side of life is yours to achieve too, with the benediction of all who find life good.[5]

On Dating

To pet or not to pet is obviously only one aspect of the larger problem of dating in general. If sex is only one very important item in the total love relationship of marriage, it is also one of many important considerations during engagement and courtship. We have already referred to the fact that everything you do now in your relationships with the opposite sex is, in a sense, preparation for marriage. Therefore, it becomes important to devote some attention to a number of additional questions about dates.

There is a tendency for each young person to think he or she is the only one who feels somewhat clumsy and awkward in asking for or accepting a date. The fact is that such inner lack of confidence and poise is perfectly normal—"standard operating procedure," so to speak, for adolescent boys and girls. Many an engaged or married couple enjoy hearty laughter together in later years when comparing notes on their respective feelings during the early weeks or months of their dating experience. Each felt uncertain and insecure compared to what he assumed was the assurance and complete confidence of the other. They later realized that they were equally awkward, but each saw this only in himself. With experience in dating one develops greater security and poise.

One reason for the trepidation which often precedes a date is that the individual isn't quite sure of just what is expected of him. A few years ago, about eight thousand high school students were surveyed in an attempt to ascertain the qualities most desirable in a prospective date. Both boys and girls agreed overwhelmingly that they enjoyed most spending an evening with someone who is

—physically and mentally fit,
—dependable and trustworthy,
—careful of personal appearance and manners,
—clean in speech and action,
—pleasant in disposition, with a sense of humor,
—considerate of others, and
—able to act his own age, not childishly.

What are the traits of which girls in this survey complained most frequently in the boys they had dated?

1. Vulgarity in action and speech—
2. Too anxious to neck and pet—
3. Reluctance to give compliments—
4. Carelessness in manners and dress—
5. Disrespect of the opposite sex.

And what were the complaints voiced most often by boys? That the girls they had dated were:

1. Too self-conscious and shy—

2. Too sensitive, too easily hurt—
3. Emotionally cold—
4. Too possessive—
5. Acting childish and silly.[6]

There is a temptation to wonder what connection there may be, if any, between the second complaint of the girls and the third expressed by the boys. What do you think? In any event, each sex, when confronted with the list compiled by the other, was in general agreement that the criticisms were fair. It is easier, however, to agree in theory than to take concrete steps to improve the impression one gives on a date. So let's try now to translate these valuable generalities into a few specific suggestions for your future dates.

Simple Courtesy

It helps considerably if, at the very beginning, a boy asks for a date in a manner which indicates that he would really very much like to spend an evening with the girl he is inviting. If he has a specific place or occasion in mind, it should be mentioned; then the girl has all the facts on which to base her answer. He should, as much as possible, avoid asking her at the last minute, as if it were an afterthought or a last desperate try after having been turned down by someone else. If, for a legitimate reason, he was unable to make the invitation sooner, it would be wise to say why, honestly. When he has no particular party or program in mind and just wants to spend an enjoyable evening with a girl whom he likes, it will make things much more pleasant if he discusses with her what she might like to do, or where she prefers to go.

Thus far, all the responsibility for courtesy seems to rest on the boy. Obviously, however, the girl's obligations are no less important. She owes it to the boy who has invited her to give him an answer as promptly as possible. If she must wait to consult her parents or find out whether or not tentative family plans are confirmed, she should tell him so, and promise him an answer by a specific time. He is entitled to a direct *yes* or *no* answer at the

180 *CONSECRATED UNTO ME*

earliest possible moment. It is unforgivable to keep a boy dangling in order to see whether a better offer turns up for that night, or to break a date already made in favor of one which seems more attractive. If the answer is yes, it should be given in a manner and voice indicating the girl really looks forward to spending the evening with him. If the answer is no, it should be as polite and considerate as possible. The only excuse for not telling the truth is that it might unnecessarily hurt someone. If the real reason a girl turns down a date is that she finds the fellow an insufferable boor or his company boring, kindness requires that she try not to be so specifically truthful as to hurt his feelings. A tactful *white lie* to spare another person may at times be justified; when it is meant to deceive or take oneself off the spot, it is never warranted.

Another dating area which calls for mutual consideration is the matter of money. How much should a boy be expected to spend on a date? That will depend, of course, on a number of things: on the occasion, on his overall financial condition, on his available cash at the moment. When two people know each other well and have dated before, they can discuss these things without embarrassment. When their relationship is not that close, the invitation itself will often provide a clue to how much the boy expects to spend. A bid to the senior prom obviously involves spending more money than an evening at the corner movie. A girl who is asked out for dinner or taken for refreshments on the way home can estimate how much she is expected to spend, by the kind of place to which they have gone, and by waiting to see what the boy orders. If the choice of place is left up to her, she can tactfully suggest several at different price ranges, letting him make the final decision.

Sometimes, when a boy and girl know each other well and have dated frequently, they may wish to split the cost of an expensive date. No hard-and-fast rule can be made on this. If the two people involved feel comfortable about such an arrangement, there is no reason not to make it. If, on the other hand, either is embarrassed, it would be better not to attempt "dutch treat" dates.

In other words, two people on a date should have mutual consideration and respect for each other as people. Neither one should just *use* the other for his own immediate purposes. What we said earlier about the difference between I-It and I-Thou relationships

**"It was a wonderful evening, Harold—
worth every cent I loaned you."**

applies to dating, too. A girl has no right to accept a date from a fellow whom she neither respects nor likes, just as a way of getting to a place or event she finds attractive. A boy should not date a girl whom he does not respect or like, just because it flatters his ego to be seen with her or in the hope of "making out."

Always Parents

Often dating creates tensions, not just between the two people most directly concerned, but also between one or the other of them and his or her parents. One way to reduce, if not altogether eliminate, such tension is to be honest with parents. True, some parents are unreasonable in their expectations, but most of them will respond with honesty and considerateness if they are approached in this spirit from the start. Parents have a right to know whom their child is dating and to meet the dating partners. This is obviously a problem more frequently involving the parents of the girl than the parents of the boy. When a fellow comes to the home of his date for the first time, he should be introduced to her parents. A few minutes in which to get acquainted make a good prelude for the rest of the evening—but *a few minutes*, not longer; he didn't come to spend the evening with her parents!

Sometimes parents will strongly object to a particular boy or girl their daughter or son is dating. There is no sure and certain formula for such disagreements. Parents are not always right, but neither are they always wrong. Adolescent boys and girls are not always wrong, but neither are they always right. Each has an obligation to listen to what the other has to say, as calmly and objectively as possible. Remember: *if* your parents are right in objecting to a particular date, it is you who stand to lose most by defying them just for the sake of asserting your own will. And *if* they are wrong, your best chance of convincing them in the long run is by patient listening and courteous response.

How about parents who refuse to leave the room or the house when their son or daughter is entertaining either a single date or several couples? There would appear to be a deplorable lack of trust in any parent who insists on remaining in the same room with a dating high school student. But the fault could be on either side: the student could have shown by previous irresponsible conduct that he hasn't earned such trust; or the parent could be too strict. Most parents will have enough confidence in their children at this age to give them the privacy of a room in which to entertain a friend or friends.

The same thing does not apply, however, to vacating the house. There is no reason why parents should be expected to become exiles whenever a stay-at-home date is planned. A responsible son or daughter will be happy to have mom and dad in the house, perhaps even in the same room for part of the evening. But the privilege should not be abused. Thoughtful parents will act their age and allow young people as much freedom as they have shown a mature capacity to use.

Curfew can be a troublesome problem. The hour which is reasonable for a date to end depends on the age and maturity of the individuals involved, as well as on the occasion. There are always a few special occasions during the year when parents can afford to be flexible about time limits. The probability that your parents will understand this depends in part on how reasonable and cooperative you have generally been.

When youngsters play each other off against their parents—each insisting that *everybody else is permitted to stay out later* when in point of fact *everybody else* is saying the same thing—they are not being fair. When parents persist in applying to a high school senior a curfew appropriate for a fourteen-year-old, they also are less than just. In some communities parents and young people have cooperated to establish a schedule of curfews for various occasions. Whether on this basis, or just privately with your own parents, it is always wise to have a clear understanding of the time limit for each date. Both partners to the date should know their respective curfews. If unforeseeable and unavoidable circumstances prevent your getting home on time, every effort should be made to telephone your parents in order to spare them unnecessary worry. When two people have different curfews, the one with the later limit should be courteous enough to abide by the earlier time.

Another frequent bone of contention between parents and their adolescent offspring is the use of the family car. On this point we shall try to avoid either elaborating on the obvious or preaching a sermon. A car is not a toy; it is power. Like all power, it can be used for enormous good or immense evil. It can increase your pleasure in dating or it can kill or maim you and your passengers. This is not just theory. Almost every week-end in a large city the morning papers bear tragic testimony to some young person who knew *intellectually* that a car required extreme care but who was not *emotionally* equal to such responsibility. If you drive carelessly or too fast, if you use the car as a place for sex activities you would be ashamed to have your parents know of, you aren't being fair to them. If you have demonstrated a capacity for responsible behavior in other respects and in previous use of the car, yet your parents refuse to let you use it on dates (consistent with the needs of the rest of the family) they aren't being fair to you. Again, the answer to tension is mutual responsibility and respect.

We have already referred to the fact that alcoholic drinks lower one's self-control, thereby increasing the danger of irresponsible sexual behavior. They also slow down our reflexes—those speedy, almost-automatic reactions which we need in emergencies. A frightening proportion of serious collisions is due to the fact that the driver had been drinking. Each drink decreases the ability of even the most skilled driver to control his car. The person who values his own life—and that of his date—will neither drive within an hour of having consumed any alcohol nor will he ride in a car if the driver has been drinking.

A few details about dating remain. There is, for example, the question of how frequently it is desirable for an individual to have dates. While no one answer will cover every person or every situation, as close as we can expect to come to a general rule is to say: as often as is enjoyable and does not interfere with the health of the individual or with his other commitments and responsibilities. It would be naive to expect parents and children always to agree on what that means specifically. But we repeat here, as we have said elsewhere: your parents will be more inclined to see your point of view on this if you have shown yourself to be reasonable and responsible in other respects; you will be more moved to consider their point of view if they have been generally disposed to treat you with consideration. In most families these problems can be worked out without too much strain. If not, it often helps to call in someone whom both parents and youngsters can trust—an older, impartial relative—a camp counselor or teacher—perhaps your rabbi or doctor.

How about blind dates? They can be either good or bad. You should know the person who is arranging such a date; he or she should know both you and your prospective dating partner. Even then, it is wise for the first encounter to be at an informal house party or on a double or triple date. After that, you have a better basis on which to judge a person. And, of course, parents are just as entitled in the case of a blind date—perhaps even more so—to meet the unknown person as the evening begins.

No One Else

Before we leave the subject of dating, one more very serious problem deserves our attention. A relatively recent phenomenon in the life of American young people is the practice of "going steady." We are aware of the fact that grammatically, the phrase should be "going steadily," but that seems to have acquired a somewhat different meaning—one degree less, we are told, than "going steady," which is one degree less than being pinned, which is one degree less than being engaged. So, in the interests of clear communication, we shall be deliberately ungrammatical. By "going steady" we mean the practice of a boy and girl dating each other exclusively—no dates with anyone else.

There are rather obvious reasons for the growth of this practice. The boy and girl involved may just discover they enjoy being with each other more than dating others. They may like the fact that they can save time and money because, not being new to each other, it is unnecessary to make an impression by going to fancy places. They may feel more secure knowing they can count on each other for dates than the boy's risking being turned down by other girls and the girl's waiting in vain for a boy to call her.

There are dangers involved, however, in going steady. When we talked in Chapter Five about the stages of growth toward love, we mentioned the level on which one becomes quite generally interested in members of the opposite sex before narrowing oneself down to just one individual. To go steady too soon means either to detour around this development or to cut it short too quickly. It denies one the much needed opportunity to test his ability to relate to different kinds of personalities before settling down with one alone.

Going steady also exposes young people to the risk of drifting, almost by inertia, into the wrong kind of marriage. After a boy and girl have dated each other exclusively for a long while, they are tempted to stop asking questions and to take each other and their relationship for granted. Even if they begin to develop doubts about each other, the boy may be reluctant to break off for fear that the girl, having been taken out of social circulation for so long a time, will be hurt more than he. A final danger is that a couple who spend all their dating time together increase the temptation to go farther than they should sexually than if each is dating a variety of partners. All of which means that while going steady has certain obvious advantages, there is a price to be paid too. Often in the long run that price by far outweighs what is gained.

So much for dating. Your ability to handle the normal problems of dating in general is a test of your maturity and of your readiness for the next stage, dating one particular boy or girl to the exclusion of all others. That, in turn, is the testing ground for the next step, engagement. And only one who has shown himself able to cope with the challenges and tensions of an engagement is ready for marriage.

For Instance

A. Linda and Mel have been dating for two years and have been engaged for eleven months. During all that time they have talked frequently about how far to go in their petting and at what point to stop. Neither has ever had intercourse; both have felt they wanted to save this for their married life together.

It is now just three weeks prior to their wedding. They have gone together for a week-end skiing trip and, after a day in the snow, a delicious dinner and a couple of drinks before a glowing fire, are ready to retire for the night. Linda is surprised suddenly to hear herself suggesting to Mel that they should spend the night together. "We've waited a long time," she says to him. "We have no doubt that we love each other, that we want to belong to each other for life. Is three weeks really going to make that much difference? Will a few words spoken by the rabbi and his signature on a certificate change how we feel about each other? Why doesn't our love and our intention to marry make right now anything that will be right three weeks hence?"

> What should they do? Why? Would the situation be any different if Mel rather than Linda had made the suggestion? Is Linda correct in saying that a ceremony and signature are less important than their love for each other? Will their future happiness together be in any way affected by the decision they make now?

B. Three years ago Louise experienced the only sexual indiscretion of her life. She had been dating Charlie for nearly a year when one romantic night, before either of them realized what was happening, their petting had resulted in intercourse. It was an extremely distasteful episode for her, one which she resolved never to repeat. And she had kept her resolution with both of the boys she had dated since then, including Earl, to whom she is now engaged. She has told him nothing of the earlier event, nor of the fact that she had become pregnant, but with the help of a nurse she knew, had lost the baby through an abortion early in her pregnancy.

As the date of her wedding to Earl approaches, she finds herself increasingly troubled by a dilemma. Shall she tell him or not? If she does, she is afraid she may lose him. If she does not, will she be able to live with herself and to feel that she has been honest with her husband? Though she has been a calm kind of person most of her life, lately she hasn't been able to sleep well because of this worry.

> What should Louise do? Why? What will be the probable consequences of keeping this episode to herself? Of telling it to Earl? Is there a perfect solution?

C. Linda's parents were very upset over the fact that she and Len had been going steady for eight months and showed no signs of terminating their relationship. It wasn't that they had any specific objections to Len; he was a nice enough boy, but they thought a sixteen-year-old girl shouldn't be dating exclusively with a boy a year older than herself. "Linda dear," they remonstrated time and again, "you're cheating yourself out of a wonderful opportunity to get to know many different kinds of boys. It isn't that you're dependent upon Lennie for dates; you've just scared off all the other boys by repeatedly refusing them, but if it got around that you are available for dates, they'd be calling you again in no time."

When Linda paid little heed to their protests, her parents finally laid down the law. "From now on," they insisted, "you may have two dates a month with Len—absolutely no more! If you want to go out more than that, it will have to be with other boys!"

Linda's tears and temper had no more effect on them than their words had on her. Finally, faced with no alternative, she promised. But from the beginning, she had no intention of keeping her word. Two of her girl friends conspired with her to have their dates pick Linda up, then they would all meet and Len would be her date for the evening. This has kept things under control for Linda at home. She feels a little guilty about deceiving her parents but comforts herself with the thought that they were unfair to her in asking for such a promise, so it's really their own fault. The possibility of her deception being discovered by them actually bothers her more than does her guilt.

> What reasons other than those given here could have motivated Linda's parents? What specific arguments might Linda have used in answering them? Who was right? Were her parents reasonable in establishing the rule they did? Was Linda wise or reasonable in her behavior? What would be the probable effect if they were to discover her deceit? If they do not discover it? Which side of the argument about high school students going steady do you think is more valid? Why?

D. Johnnie is the first boy who has seemed really interested in Gwen. They have had half-a-dozen dates together and only now, in her senior year at high school, is she beginning to overcome the feelings of inferiority and rejection she felt in the past because she was so seldom asked out on dates.

But lately there has been trouble between them. Johnnie has been insistent on petting. Gwen has said it's all right for him to put his arm around her if he wants to and a good-night kiss is also permissible, but "nothing below the neck, Johnnie, that's final!" His answer has been that Gwen is being unfair. "What do you think this is," he has demanded, "the Middle Ages? For crying out loud, every fellow I know pets with his girl on dates; am I supposed to be the only one with no rights?"

Their last argument on the subject took place two weeks ago. Since then, Johnnie hasn't asked her for another date. Tonight, however, he called, and they are to be together again Saturday. Gwen is positive the subject of petting will come up again. She hasn't changed her firm resolve, but is afraid that if she persists in refusing him, this may be the end of their relationship. To go back, after the fun of the last few months, to the lonely week-ends she formerly experienced would be dreadful.

> What should Gwen do? Is Johnnie being fair to her? Is she being fair to him? Will giving in to him assure her of his continued interest in dating her? Will persistence in refusing mean no more dates with him? If so, should she risk it? If she gives in to him, what is their future relationship apt to be like? If she does and they continue to see each other, what kind of marriage would they have?

E. Before Stan's parents went to Florida, they laid down the law that he was not to use the car after dark. They left the key with him, saying that he could drive to school or for any other reasonable daytime purpose, but not on dates at night. While they were gone, Stan could see no harm in using the car also for dates. So he did, making sure that he didn't pile up too much mileage.

Shortly after his parents returned, they discovered, through the chance remark of someone who had seen Stan several times in the car at night, what he had done. They were furious. Their first reaction was to say that he couldn't drive on any date for the next six months. Then they forbade him to date the girl in whom he was interested. "We never did like her" they insisted; "she just isn't right for you. She's loud and crude and the longer you go with her, the harder it will be to break it up. So, whether you realize it or not, we're doing you a favor by insisting that it stop at once. We're older and wiser than you; we know what's best for you better than you do yourself. If you stay away from Myra and otherwise behave for six months as we expect you to, then we'll consider allowing you to drive again on dates."

Did Stan really do any harm in disobeying his parents? Were they justified in their anger? In their resentment of Myra? Did they have a right to forbid further dating between them? To punish Stan as they did? Was it true that they knew better than Stan what was good for him? What will be the probable consequences of their order to their son? What would you do in his place?

Chapter THIRTEEN

THE STAKES ARE HIGH

LET US EXAMINE, NOW, THE QUESTION OF MIXED MARRIAGES. THIS term refers to any marital partnership in which husband and wife come from different backgrounds, either racially or religiously: Negro and White, Protestant and Catholic, Caucasian and Oriental, Christian and Jew. For present purposes we shall limit ourselves largely to the last of these, marriages in which one partner is Jewish and the other is not.

The mainstream of Jewish tradition has always been opposed to such marriages. We see this even as long ago as in Bible days. When Abraham sent his faithful servant to find a wife for his son Isaac, he warned him: ". . . thou shalt not take a wife for my son of the daughters of the Canaanites, among whom I dwell. But thou shalt go unto my country, and to my kindred, and take a wife for my son . . ."

Since Abraham gave no reason for this injunction, we can only guess about his motivation. The reasons become clear, however, when his preference is embodied as law in the book of Deuteronomy; there the reason is stated explicitly. The ancient Jewish people is told that when they come to the land which God has promised them and become acquainted with its inhabitants— "neither shalt thou make marriages with them: thy daughter thou shalt not give unto his son, nor his daughter shalt thou take unto thy son. For he will turn away thy son from following Me, that they may serve other gods."

From the very beginning, then, Jewish opposition to mixed marriage was based not on any notion of racial superiority but rather on realistic recognition of the fact that such matches posed an ominous threat to the survival of the Jewish people and its faith. Even as water always seeks the lowest level, the members of a small minority group intermarrying with the majority almost inevitably become assimilated, to the point of losing their original identity.

That this was indeed the biblical motivation for resisting mixed marriage is evident in two other books of the Bible. In the book of Ezra, general opposition to such marriages is voiced in the strongest possible terms, and those Jews who had already married Gentile wives were ordered to divorce them at once. This seems extraordinarily cruel, does it not? It reflects, however, a time of grave emergency. The Jewish people had just returned to Palestine from Babylonian exile. Ezra, their leader, found that so many of them had intermarried, and their attachment to people and faith was so weak that they were confronted with the very real, imminent danger of total disappearance. Therefore, he had to take stringent steps in an effort to reverse the tide and to insure Jewish survival.

The second biblical book may seem to contradict the emphasis of Ezra, until we inquire into its background, too. We refer here to the book of Ruth. Its heroine was a Moabite girl who married a Jewish man. There is no opposition to their marriage voiced in the book. In fact, Ruth became so cherished a figure in Jewish lore that she is believed to have been the ancestor of King David himself. A careful reading of her story will disclose three important differences from the situation facing Ezra. First, this is an instance of only *one* mixed marriage; not of so many that it became a prevailing pattern. Second, Ruth lived in a time when the Jewish people was not threatened by the possibility of total assimilation. And third, she embraced Judaism—following it faithfully during the lifetime of her husband and after his death. Her second husband too was a loyal Jew. Here, then, we see with utmost clarity that Judaism has not opposed mixed marriage out of sheer stubbornness, or because of a sense of racial superiority or pride, but because intermarriage jeopardizes Jewish survival.

Do our circumstances today resemble more closely those of Ezra or of Ruth? Unfortunately, they resemble the former. All studies of mixed marriage in the United States agree that, in the past generation, it has increased considerably. Research in the city of greater Washington showed that the rate of such marriages among Jews in the late 1950's reached 13.1 per cent. As alarming as this statistic is, it becomes even more threatening when we consider that it represented an average of the *entire* Jewish community, and that *among third-generation Jews in Washington the rate had already reached 17.9 per cent.* It was discovered, moreover, that in at least seventy per cent of mixed-marriage families in Washington the children were not identified in any way with the Jewish people![1]

While the figures themselves undoubtedly vary from community to community, and there is still much to learn on this subject, there can be no doubt that the Washington pattern prevails throughout the country: the rate of mixed marriage is increasing, and the vast majority of children born of such marriages are lost to the Jewish people and Judaism. This becomes a matter of greater concern in light of the fact that the Jewish proportion of the total population in the United States has been steadily declining. In 1937 we were 3.7 per cent of the whole, in 1963 only 2.9 per cent. If present trends continue, it is estimated that by the year 2000 no more than 1.6 per cent of the population will be Jews. Intermarriage is beyond doubt one of the factors accounting for this rapid decrease. Rabbi David Einhorn, one of the early leaders of American Reform Judaism, was more prophetic than he himself may have known when he wrote, nearly a century ago: ". . . intermarriage drives a nail in the coffin of Judaism."

194 *CONSECRATED UNTO ME*

But Why Christians?

All this helps explain why Jews have been so strongly and at times bitterly opposed to mixed marriages. The interesting thing, however, is that Christians—who do not confront the same danger of group disappearance—are almost equally averse to it. In 1956 the General Conference of the Methodist Church declared that "recent research has emphasized the importance of common cultural and religious backgrounds as the foundation of successful marriage. It is important that Protestant youth discuss this problem with their ministers before it is too late. Ministers are urged to discuss with both youth and parents the likelihood of failure in mixed marriages."[2] Three years later the Lutheran Church Missouri Synod adopted a statement affirming that "religious agreement between a husband and wife is undoubtedly one of the major factors in securing that peace and harmony that makes possible the normal functions and development of Christian family life."[3]

These statements, so typical of many others that could be quoted from both Protestant and Catholic sources, indicate that another reason for opposition to mixed marriage is the decreased probability of happiness and success. It will be remembered, we hope, from earlier chapters, that the more two individuals share common cultural background and values, the greater will be the odds favoring a happy marriage. In the next chapter we shall see that a shared religious experience can be one of the strongest positive factors producing marital happiness. In mixed marriages this positive possibility becomes, instead, a destructive one. This does not mean that every mixed marriage is doomed to failure, or that every marriage within a given religious group can count on success. What it does mean is that, in the delicate balance which determines the plus or minus of each match, mixed religious backgrounds are a serious hazard which frequently makes the difference.

The facts reveal this to be true. Whatever statistics we have indicate the divorce rate to be between three and four times higher among mixed-marriage couples than among others. In one of the earliest authentic scientific studies of marriage, Burgess and Cottrell concluded that the chance for success in marriage is eleven times greater where husband and wife agree on all religious matters than where they differ.

In an earlier chapter we made passing reference to an investigation made in 1938 by the American Youth Commission. The following table, taken from that study, reflects the number of young people in several categories who were found to come from broken homes.

Both parents Jewish	4.6 percent from broken homes
Both parents Catholic	6.4 percent from broken homes
Both parents Protestant	6.8 percent from broken homes
Parents from mixed religions	15.2 percent from broken homes
Parents with no religion	16.7 percent from broken homes

For anyone who truly understands the meaning of marriage, this should not be difficult to understand. It must be remembered—with reference to Judaism perhaps even more than other religious traditions—that religion is more than just theological belief. It also involves attitudes toward the meaning of life, frames of reference regarding sex, patterns of family behavior, idioms and idiosyncracies of language, matters of food and holiday observance, etc. A Jew who is accustomed to celebrating Chanukah and Passover would find it extremely difficult to observe Christmas and Easter instead. A Christian who had always taken Communion in church might miss such a tradition painfully. There are many subtle yet vital patterns of each person's life—no less imperative for the fact that they may be taken for granted—the absence or disruption of which can pose a serious threat to his security. Mixed marriage inevitably involves many of these.

Typical of the conclusions reached by most experts on marriage, after careful study and observation, is the following, written by Dr. Clarence Leuba, Professor of Psychology at Antioch College:

> In every marriage there are bound to be some outstanding differences in interests, attitudes and beliefs; but a marriage cannot stand too many of

them. . . . Cultural, religious or racial differences are of this sort; they are likely to have far-reaching effects on marital adjustments. . . . Where the marriage partners come from different religions, economic, political or social backgrounds, there are endless possible sources of irritation.[4]

Heart of the Problem

The point of greatest possible dispute in mixed marriage is the future of a couple's children. This is also the most serious source of grief. A child's most desperate need is the security of knowing where he belongs. The child born to a couple of mixed religious background is not likely to know this security. He will probably be made to suffer certain disadvantages by virtue of the fact that one parent is Jewish—wondering all the while why he cannot be identified instead with the other who is not Jewish—oblivious to the positive pride which comes from knowledge of Judaism and which can serve as an effective antidote to painful prejudice.

The author remembers a woman who came to him some years ago, insisting that he convert her to Judaism before she would be willing to marry her Jewish suitor. Her vehemence elicited considerable curiosity about her motives. After insistent questioning, she finally responded: "Rabbi, I am myself the product of a mixed Catholic-Protestant marriage. I know in my own blood and bones the terrible uncertainty and perplexity which afflict such a child. Under no circumstances would I ever cause such pain to any child of mine. This is why I insist that my marriage must be based on a religiously unified home!"

In addition to the insecurity already discussed, where religious unity is not achieved, there is also a probability that somewhere along the line the children will become ropes in a tug-of-war; if not between their parents, then perhaps between competing grandparents. It is extremely difficult for two families of divergent religious loyalties not to press their respective points of view, however subtly, upon their children. The love between husband and wife must be extremely strong and almost superhumanly mature to survive such potential competition. This is often the straw that breaks the camel's back of marital happiness. And the result—more often than we would like to contemplate or admit—is a confused, neurotic child.

Sometimes even intelligent parents deceive themselves on this score. While they act as if all the problems posed by interfaith marriage have been solved, their children reveal the truth; in erratic behavior when they are young, or in confidential conversation with trusted advisors when they reach high school or college age. It is not uncommon for a clergyman, psychiatrist, or college professor to hear from the children of such marriages that they detected the religious differences between their parents, and felt a subtle but devastating war being waged through and over themselves.

It is not only intermarried parents who often use their children as pawns in working out their own unresolved religious conflicts; children too have been known to play their parents off, one against the other. Several rabbis have, in recent years, been confronted with students of Junior High School age who refused to continue their religious education. Their justification was that with only one parent being Jewish, they had the right to opt for the parent who was Christian. The problem is serious and disruptive enough when it is thus expressed on a conscious level. It becomes ever so much more explosive when repressed to the level of the unconscious, where it can cause many kinds of emotional distress.

Neat intellectual solutions agreed upon in theory before the wedding often fail to stand up before the stubborn realities of daily life. Two young people romantically involved with each other, no matter how sensitive or perceptive they may be, cannot possibly know what it will be like one day to behold their own precious child, fruit of their bodies and their love. To agree in advance that a child will be reared in no religious tradition, or in that of one's mate, may seem like such a simple thing at the time. But when the child snuggles in one's arms, suddenly the problem is emotional too, not intellectual alone. Circumcision and Bar Mitzvah and Confirmation for the Jew—Baptism and Communion for the Christian—there is no way of preparing a couple ahead of time for what these rituals can mean later in the life of their child.

The writer of this volume has had two unforgettable experiences which bear on this point. Late one night he sat for several hours with a Jewish father and Protestant mother who had asked his help with the problem of religious education for their children. The discussion had been neither pleasant nor productive. As the couple was about to leave, the author asked one last question. "If you had known sixteen years ago what you know now . . ." he began. He never had a chance to finish the question. The wife turned to him and shouted almost viciously, "If I had known then even half of what I know tonight, I would never have married him!" This, if you please, in the presence of her startled husband! The disappointment and hatred so evident in her voice bespoke a frustration which was pathetic.

The other experience involved a Lutheran father who asked one day for an appointment. Sitting across the desk from the author, he recounted the following story: He had been born a Jew. Religion had meant so little to him that twenty years before, at the time of his marriage, he had glibly agreed to have his children follow the Lutheran faith of their mother. Throughout the years this had not seemed to pose any problems of grave consequence. But now he had come to see a rabbi because his son was six months short of thirteen. "Rabbi," he blurted out between tears, "it has suddenly come to me that this boy will be the first son in my family for centuries not to celebrate a Bar Mitzvah. I haven't been able to sleep for weeks since that thought first occurred to me." And the man wept copiously—almost like a hurt child.

> Had you been the rabbi in the two incidents described above, what would you have said or done? What would you have done if you were the husband in the first case? In Greece there is almost no intermarriage because it is forbidden by state law. Would this be a good solution for us in the United States? Why?

How does one convey experiences like these to a couple already in love and contemplating marriage? It isn't easy—it may even be impossible. This is where the more immediate problem of dating with non-Jews enters the picture. In our earlier discussion on dating we intentionally deferred this; it can best be considered here, in connection with the whole issue of mixed marriage.

The Stakes Are High 199

Are You Free Tonight?

There is nothing morally wrong in a Jew dating a non-Jew. It can be, however, explosively dangerous. No one decides in advance when and with whom he will fall in love. The more you grow accustomed to dating Gentiles, the greater is the possibility that when love arrives on the scene, the other member of the cast will be of a faith different from your own. You may be inclined to protest at once that you are still in high school and not likely to be choosing your permanent mate this month or next. True, but the matter is not so simple.

For one thing, there are couples who establish a romantic relationship in high school which persists through the years to the point of marriage. One can never be sure. It is still more likely that boys or girls who establish a general pattern of dating Gentiles in high school will continue that dating pattern in college too. In this connection it would be wise for any young person who seems to prefer non-Jews to Jews as dating partners to ask himself why. Earlier, we mentioned that one's choice of a mate can in some instances be a rebellion against parents. This is especially possible when the mate—or dating partner—is of a faith different from one's own. Such a choice is often the best device at hand—no less effective when adopted unconsciously—for hitting out at one's parents. Or it can be the expression of bitter resentment against being a Jew. In either case, the motive is not a healthy one, and the prognosis for a good marriage is far from encouraging.

Several studies have been made of the type of personality apt to marry out of the group or faith. They show in this category a disproportionate number of people who are "unorganized or demoralized . . . detached . . . rebellious . . . marginal . . ." This, of course, does not mean that every person contemplating a mixed marriage fits these descriptions; only that more individuals of this type than of others will eventually enter into such marital partnerships. Very often the compulsion to marry outside one's group is a symptom of general personality disorder or inadequacy.[5]

The path of wisdom then—if one wishes not to rule out completely the dating of Gentiles—is to keep these contacts on as casual a basis as possible. Let these dates be interspersed infrequently in a dating pattern which is mostly with Jewish partners. And let the first symptoms of any affection exceeding simple friendship be a warning signal that grave danger lies ahead!

This brings us back to mixed marriage. Suppose both the prospective bride and groom happen to be people to whom religion seems not to have much meaning? Can they then afford to disregard the precautions recommended in this discussion? Not if they are wise. The fact that religion is of relatively minor importance in the life of a young man or woman in the twenties is no guarantee that it will be unimportant in the thirties or forties. Religion generally means more to young parents than to adolescent or immediately post-adolescent men and women. To establish a household and family on the premise of religious neutrality or indifference is to deny, from the start, a precious area of sharing which can bring immeasurable happiness to a married couple and their children.

Just in Case

Suppose that, despite the truth of everything that has been said, two people—only one of them Jewish—find themselves in love, determined to marry? What course should they follow? The first essential is to resist the inevitable temptation to say: "We're different!" Almost every couple in this situation responds in some such manner, and the tragic thing is that they honestly believe themselves to be capable of surmounting all the difficulties and obstacles of which they are at least intellectually aware. Yet an alarmingly high proportion of these couples learn later through the bitterest kind of personal disappointment that in fact they were not different.

There is a maximum weight which every beam, even the strongest, can carry. If more than its maximum is piled on, the beam will crack and break. There is also a maximum strain which any individual or couple can tolerate, a point at which their marriage must fail because the weight they have attempted to carry exceeds the strength of their love. Mixed religious background constitutes one of the heaviest burdens for any couple to carry. Those who blithely dismiss the experience of others, who proceed with their plans to marry because of a naive confidence that they will surely succeed where so many others have failed, do themselves a grave disfavor. Dean Pike of the Episcopal Church has compared them to one who would purchase a ticket for a trip by plane on the assurance of the agent that "once in a while a plane gets through." The very first practical course for such a couple is to consider seriously the additional problems their marriage will have to carry, and to measure with impeccable honesty the quality of the love they possess.

To do this properly requires time. Here we would remind you of what was said many pages back about the test of time being our most valid way of distinguishing infatuation from love. If this is true of the average couple, it is very much truer of the couple contemplating a mixed marriage. Their engagement needs to be both longer and more searching. To succeed, they must try to be even more confident than others that they are sufficiently compatible and mature.

Such a couple would also do well to inquire scrupulously into their motives. A young man or woman who has experienced unusual difficulty with a parent or a home situation, who has been perceptibly unhappy on the job, who has followed a consistent pattern of dating members of other faiths; this person should be extremely cautious about the real, unconscious motivations which drive him toward so precarious an experiment. A marriage undertaken as a weapon to punish a parent, or to strike back at an unkind fate, or to achieve a spurious sense of superiority is almost certainly bound to fail.

If the most rigorous kind of investigation over a protracted period of time leaves a couple still convinced that they wish to proceed with a mixed marriage, they should then give serious consideration to the possibility of the non-Jew converting to Judaism. Such conversions should not take place merely as expedient devices, only to assuage antagonistic relatives or induce a rabbi to officiate at the wedding. They are valid only after a respectable course of study which convinces the prospective convert that he can truthfully accept Judaism as the religious civilization and faith by which he will live his life. In most large cities today local rabbis cooperate with either the Union of American Hebrew Congregations or the United Synagogue of America in conducting regular classes for this purpose. Obviously, conversion cannot change the past background or preferences of any individual. But if it is undertaken with sincerity, it can at least offer the couple the best possible chance for happiness in a home which is religiously unified, rather than divided. And, most important of all, it can provide in advance a setting of harmony in which children will one day be able to find the security and confidence they so desperately need.

Why do we suggest only that the non-Jew consider conversion to Judaism? First of all, because we are Jews, anxious and concerned for the survival of Judaism. Second, because most intermarried couples find, whether they plan it so or not, that they are accepted more warmly by their Jewish than their Gentile friends. A majority of these couples seem to end up as Jews socially, even if not religiously. As far as anti-Semites are concerned, the couple and their children are considered Jews even if they prefer not to be. How much better then, especially for the children, to be Jews because they want to be, because they feel gratification and pride in following the Jewish way of life.

Some of the problems involved in mixed marriage must at times be faced in lesser degree by a Jew who is marrying a person from another branch of Judaism. A Reform Jewish girl, for example, in love with an Orthodox boy who insists on a kosher home, must also expect major problems of adjustment. These cannot compare in severity, however, to the vexing obstacles in the path of those who cross major religious lines in their choice of a mate.

Our ancestors were not wrong in their opposition to mixed marriage. They knew that the survival of Judaism as well as the probability of happiness are both enhanced by marriages in which both partners are Jewish.

For Instance

A. Flora and John are aware of the fact that, because she is a Protestant and he a Jew, they must expect more than the average number of problems in their marriage. They have discussed this at length with their parents, her minister and his rabbi. They have also seen the statistics of failure and divorce among couples who have intermarried.

While not discounting this evidence entirely, they are inclined to minimize its importance for themselves. They have called their parents' attention to the fact that a divorce rate three or four times higher in cases of mixed marriage still leaves a large number of matches which succeed. Their love, they are confident, will enable them to solve whatever problems they may have to face. They feel this way particularly because of the many other cultural and spiritual values they share. Their parents have not been particularly impressed by the couple's insistence that each of them might have fallen in love with someone in his own religious group with whom he would have had less in common than they have with each other.

> Is it true that individuals in the same religious group can be incompatible in many important cultural and spiritual respects? Can John and Flora be sure they are viewing their prospects objectively? Is their evaluation of the statistical evidence dependable? If they are determined to marry, what steps would it be wise for them to take in preparation for that event?

B. Jane has been a Reform Jewess all her life. Both of her parents were confirmed in Reform temples and have sent their children to a Reform religious school. Jane has now come to her rabbi, disturbed over the fact that in the past few months she has become very much interested in an Orthodox Jewish boy.

They get along well together and have a good time on their dates. Jane is slightly uncomfortable about going into a restaurant with Eric because he keeps kosher and will eat nothing except cottage cheese or fruit salad. While he doesn't object to her having whatever she wants, she feels uneasy about eating meat in his presence. The one time that she accompanied him to a religious service in his synagogue she was upset by the fact that she couldn't sit with him and didn't understand the service. The one time he went with her on a Friday night to her temple, he tried to be polite but could barely conceal his feeling that this wasn't even a

Jewish service. They have not yet become serious enough to talk about the kind of home they would have if they were married, but Jane knows he would insist on its being kosher. This bothers her on two grounds: she doesn't see why any modern Jew should want to keep kosher, and she wouldn't begin to know how to keep such a home.

She has come to her rabbi because she has never felt so close to any of the boys she has dated; she has little doubt that if she and Eric continue to keep company, their relationship might well develop into love. What she has asked the rabbi is whether or not, under the circumstances, she should continue to accept Eric's invitations and thereby perhaps complicate her life.

> What advice do you think the rabbi should give Jane? What could she do to bridge the religious gap between Eric and herself? What could he do? Is there any possibility of their being able in the future to worship together with inspiration for both? Wouldn't it be hypocritical for Jane to keep a kosher home? Is their problem more or less serious than if one of them were a Christian? From a religious point of view, what, if anything, do they have in common?

C. Having just talked to Rabbi L., Carla and Lew are deeply unhappy and disturbed. They had invited Carla's rabbi to officiate at their wedding and he had refused. Though Rabbi L. had been polite and had tried patiently to explain his reasons, still they both felt, when they left his study, as if they had been slapped in the face.

The rabbi had told them that if they were both Jewish, it would have been a pleasure for him to accept the invitation. The fact that Lew was Christian made such acceptance on his part impossible. He said there were two reasons for this. First, he was a rabbi, committed to the survival of Judaism, and felt he could not in good conscience bring the sanction of his position and the synagogue to a marriage which in all likelihood would lead to the disappearance of the family from Jewish life. In the second place, he was so convinced of the probable failure of such a marriage that he felt he was doing the couple a favor by refusing to officiate unless Lew was first converted to Judaism. Rabbi L. went to great lengths to explain that his attitude was not based on any Jewish superiority complex and that he and his congregation would accept the marriage as valid even if it were performed by a judge.

Lew says he cannot escape the feeling that Rabbi L. considers him a second-class citizen. His own Unitarian minister was willing to officiate; why should a rabbi be so narrow?

> Do you agree that Rabbi L.'s point of view was narrow? Why might it be easier for a Unitarian minister to officiate at such a wedding than for a rabbi? What else might Rabbi L. have suggested to them? Had he in fact rejected the couple? Is there any justification for his saying that he could not officiate but would accept them after their marriage if they then wanted to join his congregation?

D. Nancy simply cannot understand her parents. From her earliest childhood they had encouraged her to accept all kinds of people as friends, regardless of their color or faith. They themselves had been very active in many civil rights organizations and interfaith projects. Nancy had been encouraged to do the same.

Yet now her parents are frightened and angry over the fact that she wants to marry a Christian. "You just don't make sense!" she has insisted. "You aren't in the least consistent! All my life you teach me democratic acceptance of everyone, yet now you want me to retreat from my high ideals. If all human beings are equal, then why isn't Mark good enough to be my husband?"

In addition to her unhappiness and anger, Nancy is puzzled by the fact that up to now her parents have never been particularly diligent in their Jewish loyalties. They have been members of a congregation, but attended services only on the High Holy Days and never enrolled either Nancy or her sister in the religious school. This too seems utterly inconsistent with their present disturbance over the possibility of having a non-Jewish son-in-law.

> Can you explain this last apparent inconsistency in the conduct of Nancy's parents? Are they in fact retreating from their former democratic idealism? Does one who is opposed to mixed marriages have a right to be active in civil rights causes and interfaith organizations? Why? What

might Nancy and her parents do, respectively, to resolve the impasse?

E. Neither Harry nor Selma had ever been particularly religious. It had been years since he had seen the inside of a church or she a synagogue. They were certain, therefore, that the religious difference between them would never be more than a technicality. They felt no sense of deprivation or loss over the fact that they were married by a justice of the peace.

Harry began to change after their first boy was born. In the beginning, the difference was subtle. He would occasionally attend church services on a Sunday morning, but would never mention it to Selma, either before or after. Within two years, however, he went to church every week without fail. Then he enrolled in a Monday night Bible class and began to bring missionary tracts home.

Selma resented this. She was never quite sure whether it was genuine conviction that moved her or just an unreasoning need to strike back at her husband, but she started to observe a few of the traditional Jewish rituals in their home. Their boy was sent to Hebrew School when he was old enough.

It was the talk of Bar Mitzvah which really brought things to a head. Selma insisted on it, Harry threatened that he wouldn't attend if it were held, and the boy felt trapped between his warring parents. At this point the child developed so many symptoms of tension that he was referred by his school for psychiatric help.

Does this sound like a real or a manufactured story? How would you recommend that the impasse be resolved? Should there be a Bar Mitzvah? Could both parents be satisfied by celebrating Bar Mitzvah in a synagogue and Confirmation in Harry's church? Can we learn anything from this case?

Chapter FOURTEEN

HOW IMPORTANT IS RELIGION?

AT SEVERAL POINTS IN PREVIOUS CHAPTERS, WHEN REFERENCE WAS made to the fact that religion has been found to be an element of importance in the wise choosing of a mate and in working toward happiness in marriage, we indicated that a full discussion would be temporarily deferred. We are now ready for that discussion.

Almost everyone recognizes the important connection between religion and marriage. Even those who do not look upon themselves as particularly religious or devout are usually anxious to have a rabbi or other clergyman officiate at their wedding. And large numbers of individuals who seldom attend synagogue services of a public nature still wish to have their wedding ceremonies solemnized in a sanctuary.

It would almost seem as if many people understand by instinct a truth which can be demonstrated by experience. The fact is that the marriages of religious people *do* tend to be more successful than those of the irreligious. The American Youth Commission study mentioned in Chapter Thirteen showed that, while only 4.6 per cent of the students born to Jewish parents came from broken homes, among those whose parents had no religion the proportion from broken homes was 16.7 per cent!

> Can you offer any immediate explanation for these figures? Why should Jewish marriages be the most successful? Does this tie in with any of our conclusions in the first few chapters of this book? Why should Catholic marriages seem to be more stable than Protestant marriages? Why should those with no religious background appear to be the least successful? Is this due to the influence of religion, or to the fact that religious persons are likely to possess some of the other personality values and traits which are conducive to a successful marriage?

There are other statistics and studies which confirm these impressions. Bishop Pike, for example, has mentioned surveys which show two-and-a-quarter times the divorce rate among couples who are not connected with either synagogue or church or who worship separately, compared to those who actively share a common religious tradition.[1] Other research indicates that a high happiness score in marriage tends to be found together with a high rating in religiousness.[2] A survey, some years back, at the University of Southern California showed that among couples belonging to the same church 68 per cent of the men were happily married; in a comparable group where neither husband nor wife was a church member only 31 per cent of the men were catalogued as happy in their marriages.[3]

The Oklahoma City Family Clinic came to similar conclusions. In attempting to reconcile 250 couples who were experiencing marital difficulties, the clinic staff discovered that only three couples were attending church when they first came for help. A very high rate of success was achieved in working with these people. It was discovered that participation together in church activities made reconciliation "almost a certainty."[4]

Why should this be so? It is commonly known that the more two people share in terms of cultural background, the greater is the probability they will have a successful marriage. If this is true with reference to such cultural interests as reading, music and art—how much truer in so significant a cultural area as religion! After all, two persons who share a quest for the essential meaning of life, who strive to comprehend whether or not their love reflects an immeasurable Source of Love in the universe—two such as these have touched as deeply in their sharing as is humanly possible. They are likely to forge between them far more durable bonds of unity than two whose sharing is limited only to man-created culture.

Dr. James A. Peterson has understood this and expressed it well:

> Religious values, when sincerely believed and made
> a pivotal part of one's aspirations, must contribute
> to marital adjustment because these are the very
> values that are most necessary for it . . . It matters
> in marriage whether a couple reach upward in their
> common interests toward that which is creative and
> lofty or whether they are content with that which is
> tawdry and inconsequential.[5]

It matters especially in Judaism. Hence the very beautiful poetry of the Jewish marriage ceremony. Hence also such statements of Judaism as that in the Midrash: "No man without a woman, nor a woman without a man, nor both of them without God."[6]

Our ancient rabbis used an interesting play on words to emphasize that the relationship between husband and wife should be sacred; which means, really, that religion should play an important role in marriage. You may already know that the Hebrew word for man is אִישׁ *Ish,* while that for woman is אִשָּׁה *Isha.* The first of these words contains the letter י , which is missing from the second; the second contains the letter ה , which is not to be found in the first. These two letters together spell out a Hebrew abbreviation for God. If they are removed from the words *man* and *woman,* what we have left in each case is the word אֵשׁ *esh,* meaning fire. From this, our rabbis deduced that when God is removed from the relationship between man and woman, nothing but consuming fire remains. Only if God is present in all they experience together, is it possible for their marriage to be truly human.[7]

Thus did the ancient teachers of Judaism express their understanding of how important religious faith is to marriage. There are many kinds of experience through which a sensitive person can become aware of God and feel a close personal relationship to Him. We sense God in the beauty of the universe . . . in a mysterious feeling of kinship between ourselves and the rest of nature . . . in our yearnings after moral improvement . . . in the excitement of discovering a new truth . . . in our intuitive recognition of cosmic purpose to which, if we will, we can contribute.

But in the love of husband and wife for each other—more than in any other kind of experience or emotion accessible to human beings—men and women come close to the divine spirit which permeates the entire universe. And in the love act which unites both their bodies and their souls, through which they initiate a new life—more than in anything else they do—a husband and wife become creative partners of God. Two individuals who are unaware of this share less in life and are therefore less firmly bound to each other than those who do.

Professor Magoun must have had this in mind when he wrote: "The child who cannot find God in his parents will not have an easy time finding God anywhere. The parent who cannot see God in the face of his child has never known God."[8]

In More Practical Terms Too

There is another level too on which religion can add much to a marriage. This is in terms of visible practice rather than speculative belief. We often say that Judaism is a way of life, even more than a system of belief. Our Jewish way of life can affect the daily lives of husbands and wives in two ways. First, if they are aware of the ideals of sex, love, and marriage which our people and faith have evolved, they can enrich their relationship by undertaking to implement these ideals in their own lives. Husbands and wives who try to treat each other with the tenderness and compassion recommended by Judaism will have a far sweeter, more loving life together than those who, though born Jews, know nothing of these values.

There is often a gap between our intellectual understanding of ideals and our emotional acceptance of them. Many of our attitudes and much of our behavior in life are motivated by experiences of earliest childhood. When these experiences were particularly painful, they were pushed down into the unconscious part of our minds. Though we are unable to remember them, they continue to influence how we feel and what we do. This helps explain why we sometimes do or say things which are the opposite of what we intended, or which seem strange even to ourselves. It accounts, too, for the fact that even a person who understands and appreciates the ideals of Judaism concerning love and marriage may not always be able to apply those ideals effectively in his own life.

Most of us are able, most of the time, to live comfortably without exploring our unconscious. We manage to keep our intentions and performance close enough in line to maintain good health and self-respect. A person who is unable to accomplish this for himself may need the professional help of a psychiatrist. Often a good guidance counselor at school, or a physician or rabbi who has psychological knowledge and insight, can either supply the necessary assistance or can tell whether psychiatric aid is needed.

It is important to remember, however, that in most cases our conduct is motivated not only by the unconscious pushing us, so to speak, from below, but also by our values and ideals, pulling us upward from above. Thus the marriage goals of Judaism can exert a most beneficent practical effect on our lives.

The second practical realm in which Judaism can supplement the lives of married couples is that of ritual. In modern life we sometimes tend to minimize the great importance of ritual. As men have developed out of animal life in the direction of greater spiritual comprehension and capacity, they have also—both consciously and unconsciously—sought to express symbolically the values and concerns which mean most to them. A valid ritual is a

212 *CONSECRATED UNTO ME*

poetic symbol, through which man attempts to express something which words alone may be unable to communicate.

Shaking hands is a ritual. Though we have long outgrown the probable original reason for this custom—a desire to show the other person that one is not carrying a concealed weapon in his closed hand—it still symbolizes our openness to friendship, our desire to accept someone else as we would like him to accept us. Saluting the flag is a ritual. If performed properly, it can say and demonstrate more about one's feelings toward his nation than many words. Putting candles on a birthday cake or giving gifts to mark an occasion—these too are rituals which enrich our lives.

As the final draft of this chapter was being prepared, two events of world-wide importance occurred which demonstrated the role of ritual in human experience. One was the inauguration of Lyndon B. Johnson as President of the United States. If, as a nation, we had wanted to be coldly practical, all that was necessary was that the Chief Justice of the Supreme Court swear in the new President and Vice-President privately in his office. Instead, an elaborate ritual was performed. Members of the Cabinet and Congress entered in an impressive processional. Clergymen of four faiths offered prayers. The United States Marine Corps Band played. In the afternoon there was an elaborate parade, which was reviewed by the President and other officials from a specially-constructed stand. All this was ritual, and the nation watched it on television.

Ten days later millions of men and women throughout the world watched another impressive ritual—the funeral of Winston Churchill. Once more, from a strictly practical point of view, a private, informal funeral might have sufficed. Instead, there were massed troops, processionals of distinguished international leaders, bagpipes and bands, trumpeters and choirs, and the slow, mournful cadence of the funeral march.

Both rituals were indescribably impressive. In poetic, dramatic styles they symbolized the ideals of the American and British peoples. The movements and motions said more than even the most eloquent of words could have captured.

The day after Churchill's funeral, James Reston summarized the value of the ceremony. Calling attention to the fact that our

American government was perhaps too practical, he wrote that the rich ritual of the preceding day in London "reminded Washington of the imponderables of life. It suggested that sentiment and history, that ideas and philosophy, are also powerful. . . . The ceremony, for a few hours, brought . . . the past and the present together, and made men here wonder whether, in this computerized modern world, they were not casting aside something from the older world that was essential to the future."[9]

This role of ritual in group life is duplicated in our personal lives. It serves as a bridge from the past—across the present—to the future. It reminds us of the imponderables, the spiritual values by which our actions should be guided. We Jews are especially fortunate because our faith provides us with a rich treasury of beautiful ritual. The most important moments and emotions in life—birth, growth, adolescence, love, marriage and death—are enhanced by rituals which grow out of our people's past and express our hopes for the future.

The sharing of rituals—precisely because they are poetic symbols appealing to the emotions—can do more to bring husband and wife together than any intellectual sharing. And the most productive rituals of all for a Jew are those through which his ancestors, for centuries, have expressed their loftiest ideals. The Jewish bride and groom associate themselves with these ideals and with the men and women who developed them when—standing before the rabbi at their wedding—they repeat words and enact a drama in which every Jewish bride and groom for hundreds of years has participated. In a sense they thereby invite all Jews alive today and all Jews of the past to share in their life together, to give it the richness and strength they would be unable to evoke by themselves.

In similar manner, after the honeymoon is ended and a couple commence living a normal life in their home, each Jewish ritual they perform together brings them closer to each other and to a rich part of their background. The couple who light their candles and chant קדוש *kiddush* each שבת *Shabbat,* who commence every meal with המוציא *Ha-motzee* thanking God for their food, who participate in a סדר *seder* on פסח Pesach, who kindle the lights of חנוכה *Chanukah* and attend religious services regularly and enjoy Jewish music and literature together—this couple makes use of an asset in their marriage which they would be utterly foolish to ignore or neglect. It is true, of course, that the performance of these rituals contributes greatly to the survival of the Jewish people and of Judaism. It is no less true, however, that they add an experience of indescribable beauty and deep meaning to a Jewish marriage.

If we do not go into greater detail here regarding the ritual wealth of Judaism, this is because we assume you are already familiar with much of it from your previous studies and from your home life. Suffice it to say that the Sabbath and every Jewish holiday have something important to add to our lives, both as human beings and as Jews. The book by Rabbi Ira Eisenstein listed in the notes for this chapter can help you to understand this.[10] But it is not enough to be just intellectually aware of what our holidays mean; only the Jewish couple who *live* their holidays, who dramatize them in their home through the appropriate rituals, can benefit from them fully.

A special word is in order here concerning the Sabbath. Jewish tradition has wisely evaluated שבת *Shabbat* as second in importance only to יום כפור *Yom Kippur*. The husband and wife who deliberately set aside one full day a week for spiritual companionship and enrichment, for sharing an active pursuit of the true, the beautiful and the good—such a couple bind themselves closer to each other and to Jewish tradition. Their chance to become finer human beings and to enjoy a more wonderful marriage is greatly increased.

All this becomes more probable if, from the beginning of their marriage, a couple are affiliated with a synagogue. Most congregations today have clubs as well as lower dues for newlyweds. To join a congregation, to attend its religious services regularly, to expand your knowledge of Judaism through its adult study program— these are among the most positive ways to enhance your marriage with religion. One of the Chassidic rabbis expressed with rare beauty the importance of religion and ritual for Jewish marriage:

> It was said that the Berditschever's wife excelled even the rabbi himself in holiness. Once she was overheard saying: "O Lord, may I be worthy that

my Levi Isaac may have the same holy thoughts
when he says grace over the bread that I have when
I form the loaves."[11]

For Instance

A. Burt and Thelma, who have been engaged for six months and
are to be married in three weeks, have much in common but differ
widely in their attitudes toward religion. Thelma has been close to
her temple since the year of her Confirmation. She graduated from
the Temple High School Department, served for a while as a
student-teacher in the religious school, and attends services at least
three times a month. Burt, on the other hand, has felt no particular attachment to the synagogue or Judaism since his Bar Mitzvah.

They have discussed in some depth the role religion is to play in
their life with each other. Burt has no objection to his wife
continuing her work and attendance at the temple, but sees no
reason why he should be expected to follow a pattern of conduct
which has no meaning for him. He feels that it isn't necessary for
the two of them to be exactly alike in their loyalties and preferences, that neither should try to make the other over into a copy
of himself. He is therefore willing to cooperate in permitting
Thelma to go to temple every Friday night if she wishes, and has
agreed to have their children eventually enrolled in the religious
school, if that remains her preference. He just doesn't want to be
bothered, however, with doing these things himself.

> Is Burt right in asserting that husband and wife should not
> try to remake each other? Does this mean each should re-
> tain only the interests he had before they met? What are
> the probable consequences in their marriage, if Thelma
> and Burt remain unchanged in their views of religion?
> What could either do to improve the situation? Are they
> likely to face the same problem in areas other than reli-
> gion?

B. Charlotte and Gerald were very much impressed by the rabbi's
emphasis on the importance of a Jewish home when they met with
him for a pre-marital conference. Though neither of them came

from an observant Jewish home, they understand the value of rituals and symbols, especially for children.

They have agreed, therefore, that after their first child has been born and reached school age, they will begin to practice some of the rituals and ceremonies of Judaism in their home. They see no useful purpose, however, in starting to do that immediately after marriage. Neither of them is accustomed to this; they feel, there-fore, that they would be self-conscious—just the two of them in their little apartment doing such things as lighting candles and chanting קדוש *kiddush* for שבת *Shabbat*.

> Are Charlotte and Gerald wise in their decision? Is the value of ritual chiefly for children? How long is it apt to be from the time of their wedding until their first child reaches the age they anticipate? What do you think will happen to their intentions in the meantime? Would it make any difference to the child whether his parents had performed these rituals before his birth or began just for his sake?

C. To Zelda there has always seemed to be something both primi-tive and confining about religious ritual. Her college courses in anthropology had shown her how many of the rituals her parents observed had originated in early man's superstitions. She had learned, for example, that the origin of Chanukah candles was probably to be found in the huge bonfires kindled by primitive men as the winter solstice approached, because, as the days grew frighteningly shorter, they feared the sun would vanish unless they coaxed it to remain by lighting magic fires.

She was determined not to expose her children to such primitive ideas. She would introduce them to the highest ethical ideals of Judaism, but none of this ritual nonsense!

She objected also because she felt that ritual tends to keep men isolated in their own narrow little compartments. If Jews would relinquish their rituals and Christians would give up theirs, she felt that greater brotherhood would prevail between them.

> Does Zelda have good grounds for her objections to ritual? Is she correct about the origins of many ceremonies in

> Judaism? About rituals keeping people apart from each other? Will her marriage gain or lose by her attitude? Will her children gain or lose? Why?

D. Charlotte and Bernard, who have just come from their premarital conference with the rabbi, don't deny the importance of the statistics given at the beginning of this chapter. They feel very strongly, however, that religion can be an important positive factor in marriage only for two individuals who feel religious.

As for themselves, they are both atheists. Their college courses in philosophy have convinced them there is no God. They felt it would have been impolite to argue with the rabbi, but in later private conversation they agreed that it would be dishonest and artificial for them to attempt to utilize the beliefs and practices of Judaism to improve their marriage, when neither of them is religious at heart.

> Do you agree with their conclusions? Why? Were they correct in not arguing with the rabbi? Can an atheist honestly practice the rituals of Judaism? Are Charlotte and Bernard justified or wise in rejecting the theme of this chapter because of their feelings about religion?

EPILOGUE: AND SO—

We reach the end of this volume. But not by any means the end of your thinking about marriage. These are thoughts which should continue to occupy you for the rest of your life, first in hopeful anticipation of your own marriage, then in intelligent preparation for your children's. We hope that this book has been of interest and value to you and that you will want to reread parts of it more than once in the future.

We have tried to alert you to the most important ingredients of a good marriage: the meaning of love . . . the importance of the family . . . criteria by which to make an intelligent choice of mate . . . factors which lead to marital happiness . . . the role of sex, both before and during marriage . . . the problems of intermarriage . . . the significance of religion . . . and above all, the immense contribution which Jewish tradition and thought add to your future joy as a husband or wife.

There is an element of risk in every marriage. No bride and groom have a guarantee that their life together will be happy. The delicate ratio between the strength of their love and the weight of their burdens is one which cannot be measured with mathematical precision. The more deliberately they attempt to temper, with sober rational thought, the overwhelming emotion which attracts them to each other, the more hopeful their future will be.

You are not making your choice of a mate now. But you are shaping your personality and values; you are acquiring new knowledge and forming new attitudes; you are making other important decisions every day—all of which will eventually add up to your choice of a mate when the proper time comes. There is always a strong bond between the present and the future. What you do today helps determine what you will be and do tomorrow. Each important decision you make is like another number placed in a long column for addition. You have a considerable amount of freedom to choose what each number is to be. Once the numbers have been listed, however, once the choices made, what you are at any given moment is their sum total. No number can be erased. They can be counteracted by later subtractions, but it is very much harder to do this than to insert the correct number in the first place. In this sense, your attitudes and conduct now have much to do with your choice of husband or wife in the future.

That choice will require the keenest intelligence, the sharpest sensitivity, the most mature balance you possess. And all these invaluable traits can be enhanced by the insights of Judaism and of science. Our highest hope in these chapters has been to supply you with at least the beginning of such skills.

No marriage is always perfect, because no human being is ever perfect. There are difficulties and tensions—anxieties and worries and quarrels—between every husband and wife. But two people who love each other maturely can solve any problem and move on together to unbelievable mountain peaks of happiness.

The reading of a book—or indeed, of many books—will not make a good marriage. The assimilation of wisdom which books may contain, however, can be of immeasurable help. We end where we began. Marriage can be the most exhilarating or the most devastating experience in life. May you think and act—now and in the future—in a manner that will make your marriage a creative joy.

Notes

CHAPTER ONE

MARRIAGE: HEAVEN OR HELL?

1. E. M. DUVALL, *Love and the Facts of Life*, pp. 78 and 81f., Association Press, 1963

CHAPTER TWO

WHAT IS LOVE?

1. F. A. MAGOUN, *Love and Marriage*, pp. 3, 4 and 7, Harper & Bros., 1956
2. *Midrash Aseret Ha-dibrot*
3. *Sanhedrin 72*
4. *B'rayshit Rabba 54*
5. *Sanhedrin 105*

CHAPTER THREE

LOVE AND THE FAMILY

1. L. NEWMAN, *Talmudic Anthology*, p. 272, Behrman House, 1945
2. *Ibid*, p. 530
3. *Ruth Rabbah* I.

4. A. B. Shoulson (ed.), *Marriage and Family Life,* p. 62, Twayne Publishers, 1959
5. A. Cohen, *Everyman's Talmud,* p. 160, E. P. Dutton & Co., 1949
6. L. Newman, *Ibid,* p. 124
7. L. Newman, *Ibid,* pp. 538–40
8. A. Cohen, *Ibid,* p. 165
9. L. Newman, *Talmudic Anthology,* p. 121
10. A. B. Shoulson, *Marriage and Family Life,* p. 63
11. L. Newman, *Talmudic Anthology,* pp. 538, 541
12. *Ibid,* p. 237
13. *Ibid,* p. 271
14. *Ibid,* p. 538
15. C. G. Montefiore & H. Loewe, *Rabbinic Anthology,* pp. 511f. Macmillan & Co., Ltd., 1938
16. E. M. & S. M. Duvall, *Sex Ways in Fact and Faith,* p. 98, Association Press, 1961
17. *Yad: Ishut,* 14:8
18. S. Goldstein, *The Meaning of Marriage,* pp. 178ff., Bloch Publishing Co., 1942, A. Cohen, *Everyman's Talmud,* pp. 167–170
19. L. Newman, *Ibid,* p. 542

CHAPTER FOUR

A FAMILY IS MORE THAN TWO

1. L. Newman, *Hasidic Anthology,* p. 45, Chas. Scribner's Sons, 1935
2. *Sh'mot Rabbah* 1
3. L. Newman, *Talmudic Anthology,* pp. 121 and 126f.
4. C. G. Montefiore & H. Loewe, *Rabbinic Anthology,* pp. 517 and 521
5. L. Newman, *Hasidic Anthology,* p. 45
6. L. Newman, *Hasidic Anthology,* p. 118
7. L. Newman, *Talmudic Anthology,* p. 126
8. *Ibid,* p. 541
9. *Ibid,* p. 540
10. L. Newman, *Hasidic Anthology,* p. 304
11. *Ibid,* p. 118
12. C. G. Montefiore & H. Loewe, *Ibid,* p. 501
13. *Ibid,* p. 501
14. A. Cohen, *Everyman's Talmud,* p. 182
15. L. Newman, *Talmudic Anthology,* pp. 309f.
16. A. Cohen, *Ibid,* pp. 180f.
17. C. G. Montefiore & H. Loewe, *Ibid,* pp. 501–03, L. Newman, *Hasidic Anthology,* p. 304, A. Cohen, *Ibid,* p. 183
18. A. Cohen, *Ibid,* p. 181

CHAPTER FIVE

OLD ENOUGH TO LOVE?

1. J. H. S. Bossard & E. S. Boll, *Why Marriages Go Wrong*, p. 101, The Ronald Press Co., 1958
2. E. M. & S. M. Duvall, *Sex Ways in Fact and Faith*, p. 73
3. J. H. S. Bossard & E. S. Boll, *Ibid*, p. 110
4. *Ibid*, p. 118
5. L. Newman, *Talmudic Anthology*, p. 272
6. E. M. Duvall, *Love and the Facts of Life*, pp. 38f. Association Press, 1963
7. S. Duvall, *Before You Marry*, pp. 10f. Association Press, 1949
8. E. M. Duvall, *Ibid*, pp. 294f.

CHAPTER SIX

HOW TO MAKE THE RIGHT CHOICE

1. *Talmud Y'bamot* 63a
2. L. Freehof, *Third Bible Legend Book*, pp. 80f. UAHC, 1956
3. L. Newman, *Talmudic Anthology*, pp. 270f.
4. A. Cohen, *Everyman's Talmud*, p. 164
5. S. Kaplan & H. Ribalow, *The Great Jewish Books*, p. 229, Horizon Press, 1952
6. L. Newman, *Ibid*, p. 269
7. *Ibid*, pp. 271 and 539
8. E. W. Burgess & L. S. Cottrell, *Predicting Success or Failure in Marriage*, p. 62, Prentice-Hall, 1939
9. L. Newman, *Ibid*, p. 269
10. J. L. Baron: *A Treasury of Jewish Quotations*, p. 296, Crown Publishers, 1956
11. L. Newman, *Ibid*, p. 256
12. J. L. Baron, *Ibid*, p. 118
13. A. B. Shoulson, *Marriage and Family Life*, p. 67
14. F. A. Magoun, *Love and Marriage*, p. 229
15. *Talmud Sotah* 2
16. L. Newman, *Ibid*, p. 543

CHAPTER SEVEN

RECIPE FOR SUCCESS

1. L. Newman, *Talmudic Anthology*, p. 269
2. J. A. Peterson, *Toward A Successful Marriage*, p. 112, Chas. Scribner's Sons, 1960

3. L. NEWMAN, *Ibid*, p. 543
4. J. A. PETERSON, *Ibid*, p. 130
5. L. NEWMAN, *Ibid*, p. 546
6. J. A. PETERSON, *Ibid*, p. 98

CHAPTER NINE

DO ALL RELIGIONS AGREE ON SEX?

1. I *Corinthians* 7:9
2. D. S. BAILEY, *Sexual Relation in Christian Thought*, p. 14, Harper & Bros., 1959
3. *Ibid,* pp. 23 and 99
4. *Ibid,* p. 63
5. MAIMONIDES, *Guide for the Perplexed*, 3:49
6. S. GLASNER, in *Encyclopedia of Sexual Behavior*, p. 576, Hawthorn Books, 1961
7. EVEN HA-EZER, 76:1
8. C. G. MONTEFIORE, *Rabbinic Anthology*, p. 510
9. *Responsa,* Prague # 199
10. A. B. SHOULSON, *Marriage and Family Life*, p. 56
11. *Ibid,* p. 64
12. *Ibid,* p. 65
13. ERICH FROMM, *The Art of Loving*, p. 89, Harper & Bros., 1956
14. *Saturday Review,* 26 September 1953

CHAPTER TEN

WHY WAIT?

1. *Talmud Kiddushin* 2b
2. *Redbook Magazine,* April 1962
3. *Nation Magazine,* 8 February 1958
4. E. M. DUVALL, *The Art of Dating*, p. 200, Association Press, 1958
5. L. NEWMAN, *Hasidic Anthology*, pp. 114f.
6. I. L. REISS, *Premarital Sexual Standards in America*, pp. 170f., Free Press, 1960
7. M. FARNHAM, *The Adolescent*, p. 127, Harper & Bros., 1951
8. M. DAVIS, *Sex and the Adolescent*, pp. 230f., Dial Press, 1958
9. L. KIRKENDALL, *Premarital Intercourse and Interpersonal Relations*, p. 208, Julian Press, 1961

CHAPTER ELEVEN

DOES IT REALLY MAKE A DIFFERENCE?

1. *Time Magazine,* 24 January 1964
2. J. HUXLEY, *New Bottles for New Wine*, pp. 218f. Harper & Bros., 1957

3. S. M. Duvall, *Before You Marry*, p. 96
4. M. B. Loeb, as reported in E. M. & S. M. Duvall, *Sex Ways in Fact and Faith*, pp. 22f.
5. L. Kirkendall, *Premarital Intercourse and Interpersonal Relations*, p. 242
6. L. Linn & L. W. Schwarz, *Psychiatry and Religious Experience*, p. 143, Random House, 1958
7. *Current Medical Digest*, January 1965, pp. 31f.
8. L. Kirkendall, *Ibid*, p. 229
9. *Ibid*, p. 218
10. R. & A. Franzblau, *A Sane and Happy Life*, p. 149, Harcourt, Brace & World, 1963
11. J. A. Peterson, *Toward A Successful Marriage*, p. 55
12. R. & A. Franzblau, *Ibid*, p. 157
13. E. W. Burgess & P. Wallin, *Engagement and Marriage*, p. 204, J. P. Lippincott, 1953
14. S. U. Lawton & J. Archer, *Sexual Conduct of the Teen-Ager*, pp. 170f., Spectrolux Corp., 1951
15. L. M. Terman, *Psychological Factors in Marital Happiness*, pp. 327ff., McGraw-Hill, 1936
16. C. Leuba, *Ethics in Sex Conduct*, p. 82, Association Press, 1948

CHAPTER TWELVE

BACK TO PREPARATION

1. L. Newman, *Talmudic Anthology*, p. 541
2. E. W. Burgess & P. Wallin, *Engagement and Marriage*, pp. 371f.
3. *Current Medical Digest*, January 1965, p. 32
4. E. M. Duvall, *Love and the Facts of Life*, p. 215
5. *Ibid*, p. 95
6. E. M. Duvall, *The Art of Dating*, pp. 67ff. Association Press, 1958

CHAPTER THIRTEEN

THE STAKES ARE HIGH

1. M. Fine & M. Himmelfarb (ed.), *American Jewish Yearbook* 1963, pp. 16–30, Jewish Publication Society
2. E. M. & S. M. Duvall, *Sex Ways in Fact and Faith*, p. 61
3. *Ibid*, p. 62
4. C. Leuba, *Ethics in Sex Conduct*, pp. 127f.
5. J. H. S. Bossard & E. S. Boll, *One Marriage, Two Faiths*, pp. 100f. The Ronald Press, 1957

CHAPTER FOURTEEN

HOW IMPORTANT IS RELIGION?

1. J. A. Pike, *The Next Day*, p. 95, Doubleday & Co., 1957
2. E. M. & S. M. Duvall, *Sex Ways in Fact and Faith*, pp. 88f.

3. J. A. PETERSON, *Toward A Successful Marriage*, p. 104
4. *Ibid.*
5. J. A. PETERSON, *Ibid*, pp. 107f.
6. *Genesis Rabbah* 8:9
7. PIRKE DE R. ELIEZER, ch. 12
8. F. A. MAGOUN, *Love and Marriage*, p. 420
9. *New York Times*, 31 January 1965
10. I. EISENSTEIN, *What We Mean By Religion*, Behrman House, 1946
11. L. NEWMAN, *Hasidic Anthology*, p. 237

Permissions

The author wishes to acknowledge his gratitude to the following authors and publishers for permission to print quotations from their books and magazines:

ASSOCIATION PRESS, New York
Duvall, S. M., *Before You Marry,* © 1949
Duvall, E. M., *Love and the Facts of Life,* © 1963
Duvall, E. M., and S. M. (editors), *Sex Ways in Fact and Faith,* © 1961
Leuba, C., *Ethics in Sex Conduct,* © 1948

BEHRMAN HOUSE, INC., New York
Newman, Louis I., *Talmudic Anthology,* © 1945

Current Medical Digest, January, © 1956

THE DIAL PRESS, INC., New York
Davis, Maxine, *Sex and the Adolescent,* © 1958

E. P. DUTTON & CO., INC., New York
Cohen, A., *Everyman's Talmud,* © 1949

FORTRESS PRESS (Muhlenberg Press), Philadelphia
Crawford and Woodward, *Better Ways of Growing Up*

227

HARCOURT, BRACE & WORLD, INC., New York
Franzblau, Abraham and Rose, *A Sane and Happy Life,* © 1963

HARPER & ROW, New York
Magoun, F. A., *Love and Marriage,* © 1956
Bailey, D. S., *Sexual Relation in Christian Thought,* © 1959

RAFAEL LOEWE
Loewe, H. and C. G. Montefiore, *A Rabbinnic Anthology,* Macmillan & Co., Ltd., London, © 1938

The Nation (8 February, 1958), New York

The New York Times, New York
"Syphilis Cases Rise" (May 6, 1962) © 1962
". . . The Day after Churchill's Funeral . . ." (January 31, 1965) © 1965

Redbook Magazine (April 1962), New York

THE RONALD PRESS CO., New York
Bossard, James H. S., Boll, Eleanor Stoker, *Why Marriages Go Wrong,* © 1958

Saturday Review, New York
"What the Girls Told," Dr. Karl Menninger (September 26, 1953)
Letter to the Editor (August 15, 1964)

CHARLES SCRIBNER'S SONS
Newman, Louis I., *Hasidic Anthology,* © 1935
Peterson, J. A., *Toward a Successful Marriage,* © 1960

INDEX

Commission on Jewish Education

of the UNION OF AMERICAN HEBREW CONGREGATIONS *and*
CENTRAL CONFERENCE OF AMERICAN RABBIS
AS OF 1965

ROLAND B. GITTELSOHN, *Chairman*
SOLOMON B. FREEHOF, *Honorary Chairman*
ALEXANDER M. SCHINDLER, *Director of Education*

Union Graded Series
Edited by RABBI ALEXANDER M. SCHINDLER,
Director of Education
Union of American Hebrew Congregations